Creative
Christmas Crafts

Creative
Christmas Crafts

AURA BOOKS

First published in Great Britain in 1993
by Anaya Publishers Ltd, Strode House,
44–50 Osnaburgh Street, London NW1 3ND

British Library in Cataloguing Data

Creative Christmas Crafts
    I. Series
    745.5

ISBN 1-85470-067-7

Typeset by Servis Filmsetting Ltd, Manchester UK
Printed and bound in Hong Kong

Contents

Introduction

For the best-loved holiday of the year, what could be nicer than making your own gifts, cards and decorations?

Originally a pagan festival, coinciding with the winter solstice in the northern hemisphere, the practices of feasting, decorating with evergreens and the giving of gifts at the end of December were encouraged by the Christian church as part of the commemoration of the birth of Jesus Christ. Now 25 December is celebrated throughout the world and is the best loved holiday of the year. Every country has its own customs and traditions, and I hope there are some decorations, gifts and festive ideas to complement your festivities.

Whenever possible, materials which are freely available have been used.

Bringing evergreens into the home is an old custom in which, traditionally, the foliage is used to represent life through the long, dark winter days. Today, this type of decoration is still hung inside or outside the home and there are one or two simple designs here which can be adapted to fill your home with festive cheer. And for the children, an advent calendar is included, so that the exciting days until Christmas can be counted off.

The tradition of the tree

In many countries, even those basking in sunshine in December, there are large decorated trees in city squares where people gather to sing carols in celebration of the Holy birth. In the home, the tree is usually the focal point of the decorations and trimming the tree has become a ritual for many families, whether it be in a sophisticated colour scheme or a riot of colour and glitter.

Bringing home the tree and unwrapping the stored-away decorations is all part of the fun, for adults and children alike. In some countries, the family makes all the decorations, adding to them each year, and even have a special day for 'cutting and sticking'. There are lots of ideas for Christmas tree trims in this book including some charming little angels, some ribbon treasure bags and some novel crocheted candles.

Whether your tradition is for turkey and plum pudding, or for roast lamb and fresh fruit, the holiday is a time for family feasts and your party table will look more attractive with some sparkling decorations. There are several to choose from here – a group of cheeky robins perched on a snow-covered log, some crocheted santa figures, a papier mâché candlestick plus three impressive-looking tablecloths for you to work.

6

Gifts and greetings

Christmas is also the time of year when we send greetings to friends, renew old acquaintances and make contact with family members who live some distance away. What better way of sending that message than with a hand-made card that will be treasured? Gifts you have made yourself will always be loved more than the most expensive store-bought presents. Something for everyone is included here – a lamb muff for a little girl, wise owl ear muffs for a boy, two amusing knitted toys plus a scented pomander and a Christmas cameo picture for appreciative friends.

Remembering Christmas

Christmas is, of course, a special time for children. Most of us remember our childhood Christmases as being full of excitement and fun and perhaps the large family gatherings with the house overflowing with aunts, uncles and cousins. Or waking up on Christmas morning to find a stocking bulging with gifts – and the certainty that Santa had come during the night.

Although present day Christmases have perhaps become more sophisticated than those of old, the traditional Christmas stocking is as much part of Christmas as it ever was. Two exciting designs are here, for you to make, and which will become part of your family decorations for years to come.

Safe and sure

The projects in this book are decorations rather than toys. Many have wire or other materials which could be pulled off by determined little fingers, so, if there are likely to be young children around at Christmas, keep all decorations out of reach.

Take care when making the decorations. Follow the instructions on adhesives and have the appropriate solvents ready in case of accidental spillage (check with Better techniques). Protect work surfaces when using craft knives, and keep your fingers clear of the cutting edge. Supervise children, especially where cutting is involved. When spraying adhesives or paints follow the instructions on the container, and always spray in a well-ventilated room.

Make sure all decorations are displayed safely and, in particular, not too close to an open fire. Many decorations, especially those made of paper, plastic and dried foliage are highly inflammable so never leave a naked flame unattended. Always replace a candle before it burns too low. Many evergreens, including their berries, are extremely toxic, so keep these well out of reach of young children.

Christmas tree candles

These clever decorations are designed for the Christmas tree but they can be used in many ways – for instance as gift tags, for greetings 'cards' – or simply tape one in each window to greet your guests.

Materials (to make 3 decorations)
Coats Anchor Mercer-Crochet Cotton No. 20, 10g each of 046 geranium (A), 0759 orange (B), 0765 light French blue (C), 0131 light marine blue (D), white (E); 1.25mm crochet hook; 43in(110cm) Offray ribbon $\frac{1}{8}$in(3mm) wide.

Measurements
Approximately $5\frac{1}{4} \times 1\frac{1}{4}$in (13 × 3.5cm).

Flame
Using D, make 10 ch.

1st row: 1 dc in 2nd ch from hook, 1 dc in each ch to end. Fasten off.

2nd row: With rs facing attach B to first dc made on 1st row, 1 dc into same place as join, 1 htr in each of next 2 dc, 1 tr in each of next 2 dc, 2 dtr in each of next 3 dc, 5 dtr in next dc, 1 ch, cont to work along other side of foundation ch work 5 dtr in next ch, 2 dtr in each of next 3 ch, 1 tr in each of next 2 ch, 1 htr in each of next 2 ch, 1 dc in next ch, 1 ch, turn.

3rd row: 1 dc in each of first 16 sts, 3 dc in next sp, 1 dc in each of next 15 sts, insert hook into next dc and draw thread through, drop B, pick up A and draw through all lps on hook (always change colour in this way), 1 ch, turn. Fasten off B.

4th row: 1 dc in each of first 17 dc, 3 dc in next dc, 1 dc in each dc to end, 1 ch, turn.

5th row: 1 dc in each of first 18 dc, 3 dc in next dc, 1 dc in each dc to end, 1 ch, turn.

6th row: 1 dc in each of first 2 dc, (2 ch, 1 dc in next dc) 17 times, 2 ch, into same dc work 1 dc 13 ch and 1 dc, (2 ch, 2 dc in next dc) 18 times, 1 dc in next dc. Fasten off.

Candle
Using E, make 2 ch.

1st row: With rs facing work 1 dc over each of 11 row ends of flame, 3 ch, turn.

2nd row: 1 dc in 2nd ch from hook, 1 dc in next ch, 1 dc in each dc, 1 dc in each of next 2 ch, 1 ch, turn.

3rd to 11th rows: 1 dc in each dc, 1 ch, turn.

12th row: As previous row dropping E and picking up C at end of row, fasten off E, 1 ch, turn.

13th to 32nd rows: As 3rd row.

33rd row: 1 dc in each dc to end. Fasten off. Make another section in the same manner.

Joining
1st row: Place two sections, ws together, attach E to first row end of candle, working through both sections work 1 dc over first row end, 1 dc over each of next 9 row ends, 1 dc over next row end dropping E and picking up C, fasten off E, 1 dc over each row end, 3 dc in next dc. Corner: 1 dc in each dc to within last dc, 3 dc in next dc and complete other side to correspond. Fasten off.

Finishing
Dampen and pin out to shape. From the ribbon cut 8in(20cm) and thread through loop at top of flame. From remainder of ribbon cut 6in(15cm), make a bow and sew to candle.

Use the candle for a gift tag. Write a message on paper, attach with double-sided tape. Thread a gold ribbon tie through the crochet

This basic pattern is for making a small bauble and those pictured are worked in stripes, decorated with ribbon. They can, of course, be made in any yarns and decorated with sequins, beads, tinsel – anything you like. The baubles would be especially nice knitted in gold or silver yarn.

Materials
Sirdar Double Knitting, small quantities of 3 contrast colours; pair of 4mm/No 8 knitting needles; oddments of gold and silver thread; ribbon scraps for decoration; washable polyester toy filling.

Measurement
Approx 2½in (6cm) in diameter.

Tension
24 sts and 30 rows to 4in (10cm) measured over st st on 4mm/No 8 needles.

Special Note: These baubles are too small to be given to babies and very young children to play with. Use as decorations only and hang on the tree out of their reach.

Basic pattern
Using first colour, cast on 5 sts.
Working in st st, work as follows:
Next row (wrong side): P.
Next row: Inc knitwise in every st – 10 sts.
Rep these 2 rows until there are 40 sts.
Work a further 4 rows.
Change to 2nd colour and work 5 rows.
Change to 3rd colour and work 4 rows, so ending p row.
Next row: (K2 tog) to end – 20 sts.
Next row: P.
Rep these 2 rows until 5 sts rem.
Break off yarn leaving a long end, thread end through rem sts, then join row ends leaving an opening, fill, close. Decorate with ribbon, adding a silver thread tassel and hanging loop.

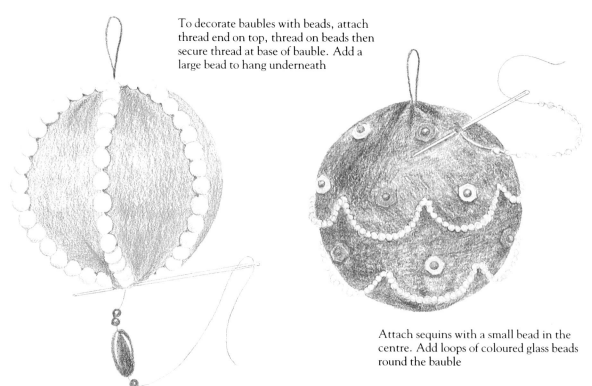

To decorate baubles with beads, attach thread end on top, thread on beads then secure thread at base of bauble. Add a large bead to hang underneath

Attach sequins with a small bead in the centre. Add loops of coloured glass beads round the bauble

Pretty angels

These little angels can be made in minutes and are perfect for children to make with a minimum of mess. Use the angels for the tree, or perhaps to make a seasonal mobile.

Materials
(for one angel)
1in (2.5cm) cotton pulp ball, painted pink
Gold foil paper
Paper doyleys
4in (10cm) piece of thick gold cord
6in (15cm) piece of thin gold braid or
 ribbon
Gold thread
Black felt tip pen
All-purpose glue

Preparation
1 Use a pair of compasses to draw a semi-circle on gold foil paper 3in (7.5cm) radius. Cut out and form into a cone, overlapping and sticking about 1¼in (3cm) at the base.

Working the design
2 Wrap a piece of doyley around the cone and stick in place.

3 Enlarge the hole slightly at the base of the cotton ball, fill with glue and push the ball on to the point of the cone.

4 To make the hair, tie a piece of gold thread around the centre of a 4in (10cm) length of gold cord. Unravel the ends of the cord and stick to the head so that the hair falls around the sides and back of the head.

5 Draw black eyes on the face.

6 Cut a 6in (15cm) length of thin gold braid (or ribbon) and form it into a figure-of-eight with one circle approximately ¾in (18mm) diameter for the halo and the other larger to form the hanging loop. Stick the centre of the 8 to the back of the head.

Glue unravelled gold cord to the cotton ball head.

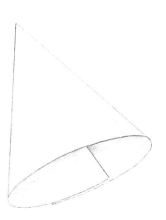

Form the foil semi-circle into a cone, glueing the overlap.

Glue gold braid to the head for a halo and hanging loop.

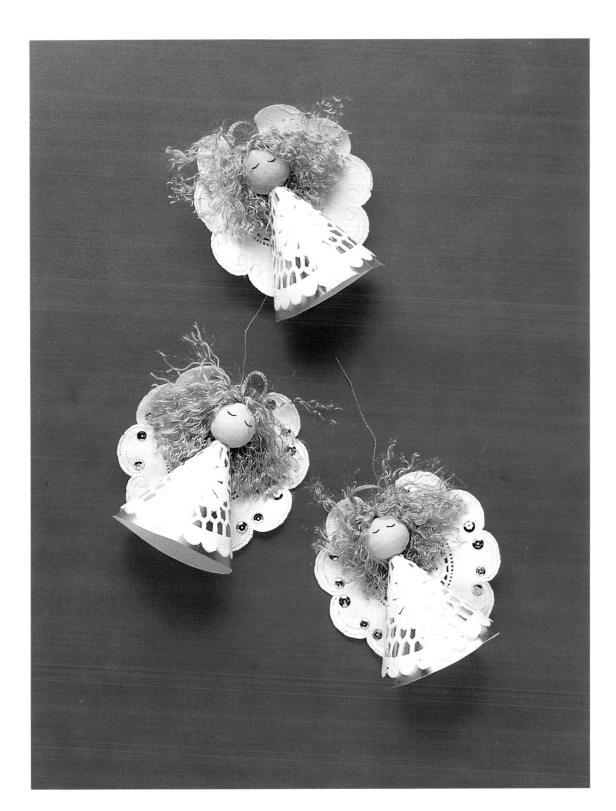

7 Cut out the centre section of a white or gold paper doyley to make the wings. Cut in halves and stick each to the back of the cone so that the wings overlap at the base and are approximately ¾in (18mm) apart at the top.

Cut the cone from blue or red paper, stick on a white paper doyley surplice and sleeves. Omit the halo and wings to make a choir boy.

Treasure bags

These little woven containers are so simple to make and are ideal for holding small gifts or sweets.

Materials

Strong, coloured paper, or laminate giftwrap to cartridge paper for the container base

Contrast papers (prepared to equal weight) for weaving

Clear craft glue

1 To make the base, follow the diagram. Cut a rectangle 6¼ × 3in (16 × 7.5cm) from paper. Draw a line ¼in (6mm) all round inside the outline. Within this, measure and mark lines ½in (1cm) apart. Cut along the lines with a craft knife. Fold the paper in half across its width.

2 Cut 6 strips of contrast paper, each ½in (1cm) wide, and long enough to wrap round the bag with a generous overlap. With the base folded, weave one strip across the next to the fold line. Continue weaving across the back. Weave in the

Cut along
the marked lines

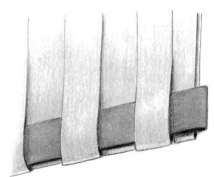

Cut long strips of contrast paper and weave them round the folded base piece

Draw this diagram on strong, coloured paper

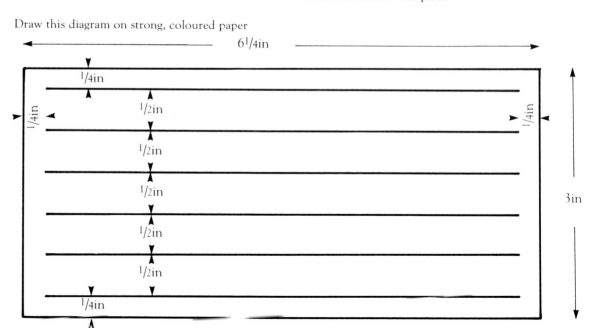

ends securely into the inside and outside of the bag. Trim the excess strip so that the ends do not show on the outside. Continue weaving in the same way with 4 more strips.

Handle
3 To make the handle, cut the remaining strip to 8in (20cm) long and weave each end into the pattern at the centre on the insides of the bag. Secure with glue.

Christmas tree skirt

Finish the tree decorations with these festive frills. A pretty, but practical tree skirt will hide unsightly pots or stands and provide a perfect backdrop for your pile of presents.

Materials
1yd (90cm) of 36in (90cm) printed cotton
½ yd (45cm) of red cotton fabric
15½in (39cm) touch-and-stick fastening

Making the skirt
1 To cut the circle for the tree skirt, first fold the main fabric in quarters to form a square of four layers. Pin one end of a length of thread 18in (45cm) long to the folded corner. Pivoting from this point mark off the radius of the skirt. Cut along this curved line through all layers.

2 With the fabric still folded in four, measure 1½in (4cm) from the folded corner down either side. Draw a line between the marked points. Cut along this line through all layers to make the top hole.

3 Open out circle of fabric and cut skirt from outside edge to centre hole along one of the creases. Narrow hem the centre hole, turning the edge under ¼in (6mm) twice to encase the raw edge. Turn the side edges under ½in (1cm) and press. Then pin strips of fastening down both side edges and machine-stitch in place.

4 Cut the red cotton into 2½in (6cm) wide strips and then sew them end to end to form one long strip. Fold this in half lengthways with wrong sides together, and gather-stitch along the raw edges. Pull up so that the frill is approximately half its original length.

5 With right sides together, pin the gathered frill to the outside edge of the skirt. Adjust gathers as necessary and machine-stitch. Press the seam allowance towards the skirt and then edge-stitch to the skirt base.

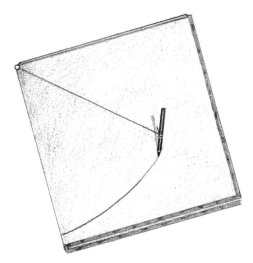

Fold the fabric into four
and mark off the radius of the skirt.

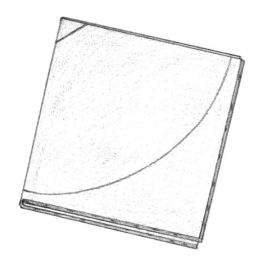

Draw a line across the folded corner.

Deck the tree

These pretty glittering Christmas tree ornaments are so easy to make that you could work several in an evening, but they'll last for many Christmases to come.

Materials

Miniature metal ornaments with punched holes

Anchor stranded cottons as follows: one skein each of 46 red, 304 orange, 291 yellow, 289 pale yellow, 139 dark blue, 160 pale blue, 230 green, 01 white.

Working the embroidery

Using three strands of cotton, work the designs following the charts and keys.

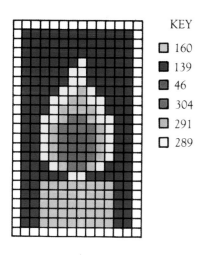

KEY
- ☐ 160
- ■ 139
- ▨ 46
- ▨ 304
- ▨ 291
- ☐ 289

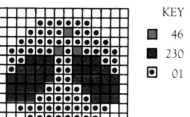

KEY
- ▨ 46
- ■ 230
- ◉ 01

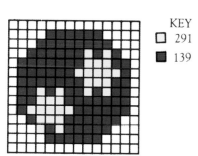

KEY
- ☐ 291
- ■ 139

For extra glitter, work the stitches in metallic threads or add a few tiny metallic beads, sewing them to the stitches afterwards.

Use the motifs for other Christmas embroidery

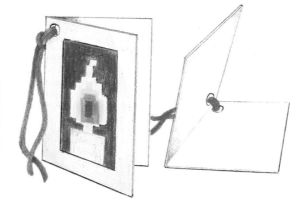

Presents galore

Tree cloths are both pretty and practical and this one with its border of brightly-wrapped presents is sure to get everyone in a festive mood. This is a pattern you'll find other uses for on Christmas embroideries – such as a party tablecloth with matching napkins.

Materials
Piece of green Binca fabric, 44in (112cm) square, 11 threads to 1in (2.5cm)
Anchor stranded cottons in assorted bright colours, 15 skeins.

Preparation
1 Measure and mark a line 3in (7.5cm) from the fabric edge all round. Use basting stitches which can be unpicked afterwards, or chalk pencil.

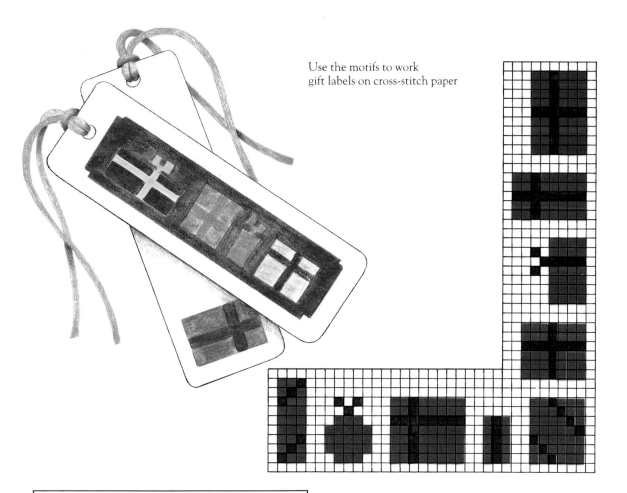

Use the motifs to work
gift labels on cross-stitch paper

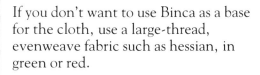

If you don't want to use Binca as a base
for the cloth, use a large-thread,
evenweave fabric such as hessian, in
green or red.

Working the embroidery
2 Beginning at one corner and referring to
the chart, embroider a border of presents
along one edge on the marked line. Use six
strands of thread together and vary the
colours at random as you work; make the
colour of each present different from the
ones next to it, with the ribbons on the
presents in contrasting colours.

3 At the next corner, work the next present
at right angles to the one just stitched, still
working on the marked line.

4 Continue working repeats of the pattern
until a border has been worked round the
cloth.

Finishing
5 Fold under ½in (1cm) all round the
cloth, press and baste in place. Set the
sewing machine to narrow zigzag stitch, and
stitch the hem. If you prefer, apply a border
of red bias binding to neaten the edges.
Alternatively, sew 1in (2.5cm)-wide gold
polyester/Lurex ribbon to the hem.

Use the gift motifs on cross-stitch paper
to make special Christmas decorations
or unusual gift labels. Work a row of
three or four for a hand-made Christmas
card. You could also use them as a
border for a Christmas buffet cloth
instead of the holly leaves. If you're
feeling adventurous, work the motif
on four pieces of plastic canvas to be
built up into a three-dimensional
Christmas decoration. Decorate with
beads.

21

Decorative boots

Little Christmas tree decorations like these boots are just big enough to take small gifts – such as lipstick, a small bottle of perfume, coins, etc. Use felt and scraps of lace or an attractive Christmas print fabric.

Materials
(for red and green boots)
Felt 4in (10cm) square in red and green
Scraps of dark green felt
Small amounts of coton perle in blue, white
   and pale green
Gold thread
Gold beads
Small length of narrow red ribbon

Preparation
1 Trace off and transfer the boot shape twice to fit into each square of felt. Cut out with sharp scissors.

2 Trace off and transfer the small ivy leaves to the dark green felt and cut out.

3 Mark the lines of embroidery on the red boot and the position of the ivy leaves and the trails on one side of the green boot.

Working the embroidery
4 On the red boot, work the detached chain stitches along the top in white, with French knots in blue. Work the detached chain stitches along the bottom edge of the boot in blue, with gold beads centred on each. Work running stitches in the zig-zag pattern in blue, then lace gold thread through each stitch. Work small, double cross stiches in white above and below the zig-zag line. Blanket-stitch the top edges in blue. Work both sides of the boot in the same way.

5 On the green boot, place the ivy shapes in position and pin. Using pale green coton perle work stem stitch for the trails. Attach the leaves to the boot with long straight stitches to make the veins. Oversew a length of red ribbon just below the top edge. Work both sides of the boot in the same way.

Making up the boots
6 Baste the boot sides together, right side out. Machine-stitch close to the edge (or work buttonhole stitch).

7 Stitch a short length of gold thread at the back seam for a hanger.

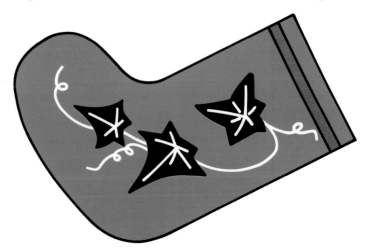

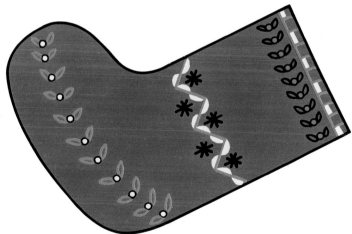

Christmas cones

For many people, the most enjoyable part of Christmas preparations is that of dressing the tree. These pretty cones are simple to make and you can vary the colour scheme of the flowers and ribbons to suit your holiday décor.

Materials
Quick-drying glue (or a glue-gun)
Gold spray paint
Gold gift ribbon
Gold-edged, red grosgrain ribbon, ½in
   (1cm) wide

Dried flowers and grasses
Fir cones
Red cluster-flowered strawflowers
   Helichrysum italicum
Canary grass *Phalaris*
Selection of other dried grasses

Preparation
1 Clean the cones and leave in a warm
place to open.

2 Place some cones and grasses inside a
large cardboard box and spray them
with gold spray paint.

3 Stand a gold-painted cone in the lid of
the spray can (to hold it in position) and
apply some glue to the top.

4 Arrange two 4in (10cm)-long pieces of
gold gift ribbon at right angles on the
glue. Leave to dry.

Tartan cones
This is just one of the variations that
can be worked with the basic
technique.

   Do not spray the cones – leave
them in their natural state. Cut 2
pieces of ½in (1cm)-wide taffeta
tartan ribbon and glue to the top of
the cone at right angles. When dry,
cut 8in (20cm) lengths of 1in (2.5cm)-
wide tartan ribbon and glue loops to
the tops of the cones. Decorate with
red flowers, small larch cones and
natural grasses.

   Tartan cones look particularly
effective if large bows of wide,
matching tartan ribbon are tied to
the Christmas tree branches.

5 Cut an 8in (20cm) length of gold-edged
grosgrain ribbon and fold to make a
loop. Glue to the cone with 1in (2.5cm)
ends protruding each side.

6 Glue pieces of grasses and strawflowers
to cluster round the cone on top of gold
ribbon.

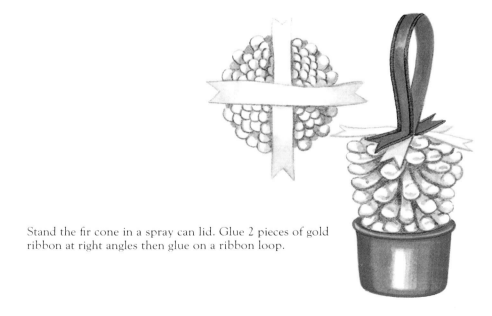

Stand the fir cone in a spray can lid. Glue 2 pieces of gold
ribbon at right angles then glue on a ribbon loop.

Stars and moons

These decorations are based on florists' dry foam and, once covered with pasted paper and painted, they are hard-wearing and will last for many years. Children will enjoy helping to make them.

Materials
Block of florists' brown foam
Small balls of florists' brown foam
Florists' stub wires
Newspaper torn into small pieces
Tissue paper
Mixed wallpaper paste
Thin cardboard
PVA adhesive
Spray silver paint

STARS AND CRESCENTS
Preparation
1 Cut slices of foam from the block. Using a star-shaped and crescent pastry cutters, cut shapes.

2 Paste small pieces of tissue all over the stars and crescents, on both sides. Leave to dry.

3 Apply 3 layers of tissue, leaving each to dry before working the next. Use very narrow strips between the star points to keep the shape.

4 When the shapes are dry, spray with silver paint. Leave to dry, then spray the other side.

FULL MOONS
5 Work the foam balls in the same way, applying 3 layers of pasted tissue. Before the last layer is applied, cut small stars from thin card and stick them to the ball. Apply the last layer of pasted tissue, pressing the paper firmly on to the star shapes to show them in relief.

6 Spray-paint the balls silver.

Cut slices from the block. Cut stars with a pastry cutter.

Finishing
7 Cut small pieces of stub wire, bend into U-shapes. Bind the wire ends with narrow strips of pasted tissue. Leave to dry. Cut slits in the top of each of the ornaments, spread glue on the wrapped wire ends and push into the slit.

Star-shaped cutters
These are available with either five or six points. Crescents and stars could also be cut by hand.

Santa doll

A jolly little Christmas doll that looks festive in yuletide arrangements, or could be hung on a ribbon from the tree. You could also use several on a Christmas ring.

Materials

1 ball (20g) Coats Chain Mercer-Crochet Cotton No. 20 each of 469 geranium (A), 625 light beige (B), white (C), black (D); 1.25mm crochet hook; washable polyester toy filling.

Measurements

5¹/₂in (14cm) high.

Tension

First 5 rows of coat measure ⁵/₈in (1.5cm).

Before commencing and using A work 2 lengths of 6 ch and leave aside for sleeves.

Coat (back and front alike)

Using C, make 28 ch.

1st row: (ws) 1 dc in 2nd ch from hook, 1 dc in each ch to end, 4 ch, turn.

2nd row: Miss first 2 dc, 5 tr in next dc, remove lp from hook, insert hook in first tr of tr gr and draw dropped lp through (popcorn st made referred to as pc st), *2 ch, miss 1 dc, a pc st in next dc; rep from * ending with 1 ch, miss 1 dc, 1 tr in last dc, 1 ch, turn.

3rd row: 1 dc in first tr, 1 dc in next 1-ch sp, 2 dc in each 2-ch sp, 1 dc in last sp, 1 dc in 3rd of 4 turning ch. Fasten off.

4th row: With rs facing attach A to first ch on other side of foundation ch, 3 ch, 1 tr in each of next 26 foundation ch, 1 ch, turn.

5th row: 1 dc in each tr, 1 dc in 3rd of 3 ch, 2 ch, turn.

6th row: Miss first dc, 1 tr in each dc to within last 2 dc, leaving last lp of each on hook work 1 tr in each of next 2 dc, thread over and draw through all lps on hook (a joint tr made), 1 ch, turn.

7th row: 1 dc in each tr, 2 ch, turn.

Rep last 2 rows 3 times more turning with 3 ch at end of last row instead of 2 ch.

14th row: Miss first dc, 1 tr in each dc, 7 ch, turn.

15th row: 1 dc in 2nd ch from hook, 1 dc in each of next 5 ch (first sleeve), 1 dc in next tr, 2 dc in next tr, 1 dc in each of next 15 tr, 2 dc in next tr, 1 dc in 3rd of 3 turning ch, attach one 6 ch length previously made, 1 dc in each of next 6 ch (2nd sleeve), 3 ch, turn.

16th row: Miss first dc, 1 tr in each of next 8 dc, 2 tr in next dc, 1 tr in each of next 13 dc, 2 tr in next dc, 1 tr in each of next 9 dc, 1 ch, turn.

17th row: 1 dc in each of first 11 tr, 2 dc in next tr, 1 dc in each of next 11 tr, 2 dc in next tr, 1 dc in each of next 11 sts, 3 ch, turn.

18th row: Miss first dc, 1 tr in each of next 12 dc, 2 tr in next dc, 1 tr in each of next 9 dc, 2 tr in next dc, 1 tr in each of next 13 dc, 1 ch, turn.

19th row: 1 dc in each of first 15 tr, 2 dc in next tr, 1 dc in each of next 7 tr, 2 dc in next tr, 1 dc in each of next 15 sts, 3 ch, turn.

20th row: Miss first dc, 1 tr in each of next 16 dc, 2 tr in next dc, 1 tr in each of next 5 dc, 2 tr in next dc, 1 tr in each of next 17 dc. Fasten off.

Sew back and front together leaving lower edge and ends of sleeves open.

Cuff

1st row: With rs facing attach C to one underarm seam and work 20 dc evenly over row ends of sleeves, 1 sl st in 1st dc.

2nd row: 3 ch, 4 tr in same place as sl st, remove lp from hook, insert hook in 3rd of 3 ch and draw dropped lp through (a starting pc st made), *2 ch, miss 1 dc, a pc st in next dc; rep from * ending with 2 ch, 1 sl st in 1st pc st.

3rd row: 2 dc in each sp, 1 sl st in 1st dc. Fasten off.

Complete other sleeve in same manner.

Front trimming

Using C, make 32 ch.

1st to 3rd rows: As 1st to 3rd row of coat.

Belt

Using D, make 47 ch.

1st row: 1 dc in 2nd ch from hook, 1 dc in each ch, 1 ch, turn.

2nd row: 1 dc in each dc. Fasten off.

Buckle

Using C, make 6 ch, 1 dtr in 5th ch from hook, 1 dtr in next ch. Fasten off.

Head (back and front alike)

Using B. make 2 ch. Mark beg of each row with a coloured thread.

1st row: 6 dc in 2nd ch from hook.

Hat

Using C, make 40 ch and, being careful not to twist ch, work 1 sl st in 1st ch.

1st row: 1 dc in same place as sl st, 1 dc in each ch, sl st in 1st dc.

2nd and 3rd rows: As 2nd and 3rd rows of cuff.

4th row: With rs facing attach A to same place as last sl st, 3 ch, 1 tr in each dc, 1 sl st in 3rd of 3 ch.

5th row: 3 ch, 1 tr in each of next 2 tr, *a joint tr over next 2 tr, 1 tr in each of next 3 sts; rep from * omitting 3 tr at end of last rep, sl st to 3rd of 3 ch.

6th row: 3 ch, 1 tr in next tr, *a joint tr over next 2 sts, 1 tr in each of next 2 sts; rep from * omitting 2 tr at end of last rep, 1 sl st in 3rd of 3 ch.

7th row: 3 ch, *a joint tr over next 2 sts, 1 tr in next st; rep from * omitting 1 tr at end of last rep, 1 sl st in 3rd of 3 ch.

8th to 10th rows: 3 ch, 1 tr in each st, 1 sl st in 3rd of 3 ch.

11th row: 2 ch, 1 tr in next st, (a joint tr over next 2 sts) 7 times, 1 sl st to 1st tr.

12th row: 1 dc in same place as sl st, 1 dc in each st, 1 sl st in 1st dc. Fasten off.

13th row: Attach C to same place as last sl st, 3 ch, a starting pc st in same place as join, 1 ch, miss 3 dc, 1 pc st in next dc, 1 ch, 1 sl st in first pc st. Fasten off.

Beard

Using C, make 28 ch.

1st row: 1 sl st in 8th ch from hook, 9 ch, 1 sl st in next ch, 10 ch, 1 sl st in next ch, 11 ch, 1 sl st in next ch, 12 ch, 1 sl st in next ch, 13 ch, 1 sl st in next ch, 14 ch, 1 sl st in next ch, (15 ch, 1 sl st in next ch) 5 times, 14 ch, 1 sl st in next ch, 13 ch, 1 sl st in next ch, 12 ch, 1 sl st in next ch, 11 ch, 1 sl st in next ch, 10 ch, 1 sl st in next ch, 9 ch, 1 sl st in next ch, 8 ch, 1 sl st in next ch, 7 ch, 1 sl st in next ch. Fasten off.

Dampen and pin all pieces out to shape.

Finishing

Thread belt through dtrs of buckle and sew front trimming and belt to coat. Sew head sections together stuffing lightly. Stuff hat lightly and sew hat and beard to head. Sew head in position to coat.

2nd and 3rd rows: 2 dc in each dc.

4th and 5th rows: 1 dc in each dc.

6th row: (2 dc in next dc, 1 dc in each of next 2 dc) 8 times – 32 dc.

7th row: (2 dc in next dc, 1 dc in each of next 3 dc) 8 times – 40 dc.

8th row: 1 dc in each dc.

9th row: 1 dc in each dc, sl st in next dc. Fasten off.

Christmas boxes

Tie these dainty little parcels to your tree for an original decoration – they can be made in colours to match your party scheme.

Materials (to make 3 decorations)
30g Coats Anchor Mercer-Crochet Cotton No. 20 main colour (M); 10g contrast colour (C); 1.25mm crochet hook; 1^1/$_8$yd (1m) Offray ribbon ^{1}/$_8$in (3mm) wide; 24 small silver beads; foam rubber pieces cut to 2^1/$_2$ x 1^1/$_2$ x 1^1/$_4$in (6.5 x 4 x 3.5cm).

Measurements
2^1/$_2$x1^1/$_2$x1^1/$_4$in(6.5x4x3.5cm).

Tension
First 5 rows measure ^{1}/$_8$in(1cm).

Main Section
Using M, make 20 ch.
1st row: 1 dc in 2nd ch from hook, 1 dc in each ch to end, 1 ch, turn.
2nd to 16th rows: 1 dc in each dc, 1 ch, turn.
17th row: 1 dc in each of first 18 dc, 3 dc in next dc, 1 dc over each of next 15 row ends, 1 ch, turn.
18th row: 1 dc in each of first 35 dc, 2 dc in next dc, 1 dc over each of next 16 row ends, 1 ch, turn.
19th row: 1 dc in back lp of each dc, 1 ch, turn.
20th to 47th rows: As 2nd row.
48th row: 1 dc in each dc, turn. Fasten off.
49th row: Miss first 17 dc on previous row,

attach thread to back lp of next dc, 1 dc in same place as join, 1 dc in back lp of each of next 18 dc, 1 ch, turn.
50th to 65th rows: As 2nd row.
66th row: 1 dc in each dc. Fasten off.

Base
Work as main section for 1 row.
2nd to 28th rows: As 2nd row of main section.
29th row: As 48th row of main section.

Trimming
Using C make 20 ch.
1st row: *3 tr in 4th ch from hook, 3 tr in each of next 13 ch, sl st to first ch, 20 ch; rep from * 3 times more omitting 20 ch at end of last rep. Fasten off.
Make 2 lengths of 95 ch each and 2 lengths of 75 ch each. Starch trimming, pull into shape.

Finishing
Sew main section into box shape. Glue paper to sides of foam pieces. Sew on crochet. Brush lightly with starch. Fold 8in (20cm) lengths of ribbon, sew to one corner of each box to form loops. Decorate boxes with trimmings, beads and ribbons.

Pretty pomanders

Hang aromatic dried oranges studded with cloves in the wardrobe for a natural perfume. Pomanders are traditional presents, particularly at Christmas, and their spicy scent makes them a household favourite.

Materials
Tape, ¾in (18mm) wide
Thin skinned oranges
Whole cloves
1tsp (5ml) ground cinnamon
1tsp (5ml) ground allspice
2oz (60g) orris root powder
Double-edged lace, ¾in (18mm) wide, 20in (50cm) long
Embroidered ribbon ⅜in (9mm) wide, 22in (56cm) long
Pearlized glass-headed pins

Preparation
1 Cut and pin tape to go round the orange, a second strip at right angles to the first, to quarter it. Pierce holes in the orange ¼in (6mm) apart. Push cloves into the holes to fill the quarter sections between the tapes. Remove the tapes.

2 Mix the orris root powder, allspice and cinnamon together in a plastic bag. Toss the orange in the mixture inside the bag. Remove and shake off excess powder.

3 Wrap the orange in tissue paper and leave in a dry, warm place for 2–3 weeks, to dry out.

Making the pomander
4 Cut the lace in half. Wrap each piece round the orange in the channels left by the tape. Overlap the lace ends and pin or glue to secure.

5 Beginning at the top, wrap the ribbon round the pomander placing it centrally over the lace. Pin or glue at the top and the cross-over point at the base. If the pomander is to be hung, form a loop at the top with ribbon and hold in place with glass-headed pins.

Pin tape round the orange, push cloves into the pierced holes. After tossing the orange in orris powder and spices, wrap and leave to dry

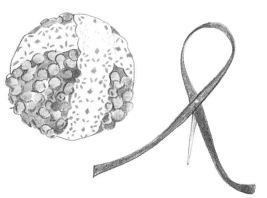

Tape lace and pin ribbons round the orange. Make a ribbon loop to pin to the top if the pomander is to be hung

Advent calendar

*Countdown to Christmas with this easy-to-make advent calendar.
A mixture of sweets and little gifts tied to the numbered rings
ensures a special little surprise every day.*

Materials
17 × 24½in (43 × 62cm) red felt
12½ × 28½in (31 × 73cm) green felt
Brown felt square
Set of stencil numerals
Gold fabric paint
Packet of Bondaweb
1½yd (1.40m) of ⅛in (3mm)-wide ribbon
24 brass curtain rings
1yd (90cm) wide satin ribbon
20in (50cm) dowel ½in (1cm) diameter

Making the calendar
1 Take the red felt background and turn
one end and both sides under ¾in (2cm)
then top-stitch ½in (1cm) from the edge.
Turn the remaining (top) edge under 1½in
(4cm) and machine-stitch 1in (2.5cm)
from the edge to form a casing.

2 From the green felt cut 3 tree shapes as
shown in the diagram. The first has a
12½in (31cm) base. The middle shape has
an 11in (28cm) base whilst the top
triangle has an 8½in (20.5cm) base with
two equal sides 6½in (16.5cm).

3 Place the largest tree piece on the
background 2½in (6cm) from the bottom
edge. Then add the middle and top
triangle overlapping each other so that
the top of the tree is 2in (5cm) below the
top edge of the background.

4 Before bonding and stitching in place,
carefully stencil the numbers 1–24 in gold
paint randomly scattered on all three tree
sections. Then attach the tree shapes to

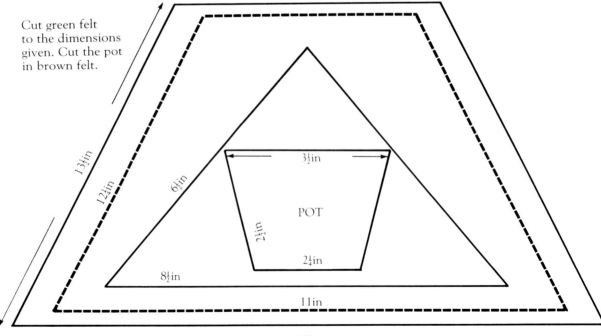

Cut green felt
to the dimensions
given. Cut the pot
in brown felt.

13½in

12½in

6½in

3½in

POT

2½in

8½in

2¼in

11in

12½in

the background with Bondaweb and a large machine-stitch around the outer edges to secure.

5 Cut out and add the brown felt tree pot. Bond in place and then machine-stitch to secure.

6 Hand sew a brass curtain ring below each date from which to hang the daily surprises. It is now ready to add the individually wrapped gifts, tied in place with ribbon bows.

7 To hang the calendar, cut the wide ribbon into two halves, fold and stitch one end of each to form a loop. Insert the dowel through the top casing, adding a ribbon loop to either end. Then tie the remaining ribbon ends into a decorative bow.

Christmas garland

*Fresh foliage garlands shrivel quickly in warm rooms
but florists can provide artificial garlands that look almost real
and last from year to year.*

Materials
Artificial fir garland
Black stub wires
Black reel wire
6yd (5.50m) of crushed, red paper ribbon

Dried material
Fir cones
Fir tree bark
Nuts, nut cases
Lichens or moss

Preparation
1 Wire all the cones, nuts and nut cases
and make bundles of the bark, twisting a
stub wire round them.

2 Divide the lichen and mount into
bunches.

3 Decide on the position of the finished
garland and offer it up. Mark the position
of the fixing points and wire in loops of
binding wire at these places.

Working the design
4 Spread out the garland and distribute
the wired decorations evenly along its
length. Secure them to the garland by
twisting the two mounting wires around
the garland.

5 Trim off the surplus wire and fold back
the ends to prevent them from scratching
your hands or furnishings.

6 Tie a large bow for the centre and 2
smaller ones for the corners. Wire them
on.

7 Divide the remaining ribbon lengthways into 2 narrow widths. Keep back 2 pieces for the garland ends. Make small bows with the rest and distribute them along the garland.

8 Hang the garland in position and tie ribbons around the hanging ends.

On Christmas morning, wire small red apples, clementines and bunches of cinnamon sticks and add them to the garland for extra colour.

Star bright

Make a Victorian-style patchwork star in three different fabrics
to hang up as an ornament.
Change the fabrics to baby prints to make an alternative to a mobile,
or small Christmas fabrics for a festive decoration.
The points are finished with crystals and pearls.

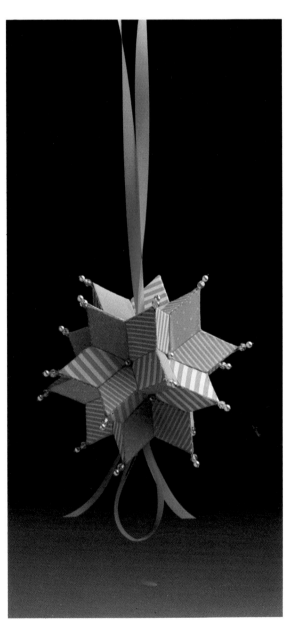

Materials

1¼in (3cm) lozenge diamond patchwork
   template
Card 15 × 8in (38 × 20cm)
30 × 5in (76 × 12.5cm) each of three print
   fabrics
Matching sewing thread
Fabric adhesive
1¼yd (1.10m) of ⅜in (9mm)-wide ribbon
20 pins
Ten matching pearl beads
20 pearl beads
20 crystal beads

To make the star

1 Using the template, cut out sixty
diamonds from card.

2 Place fabric pieces wrong side up. Mark
round diamond template 20 times on each
fabric, allowing a ½in (1cm) margin all
round each one. Cut out the diamonds.

3 Place each fabric diamond right side down
and stick card diamond centrally to each
piece. Carefully pull raw edges over card
edge and stick to wrong side.

4 Mixing the fabrics, stitch five diamonds
together to form a rosette. To sew the
diamonds together, place with right sides
together and work along one side with
hemming stitch. Open out. Hem third
diamond to second diamond and repeat,
until five diamonds are joined together.

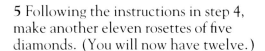

5 Following the instructions in step 4, make another eleven rosettes of five diamonds. (You will now have twelve.)

6 Stitch a single pearl bead into centre of ten rosettes.

7 Cut two 12in (30cm) lengths of ribbon. Match together. Fold in half to form loops, push ends through centre of one plain rosette and fasten on the wrong side. This will be the base rosette.

8 Form a loop with the remaining ribbon, push through centre of last plain rosette and fasten on wrong side. This will be the top rosette.

9 Take the base rosette and sew a rosette to each pair of sides. Then sew the rosettes together round the side edges. Repeat, to make up the top rosette in the same way. Note: you will now have to sew from the outside.

11 Sew the top and base halves together, along the remaining free edges, again using small hemming stitches.

12 Thread a pearl bead and then crystal bead onto each pin and pin into each of the twenty points in turn on the star.

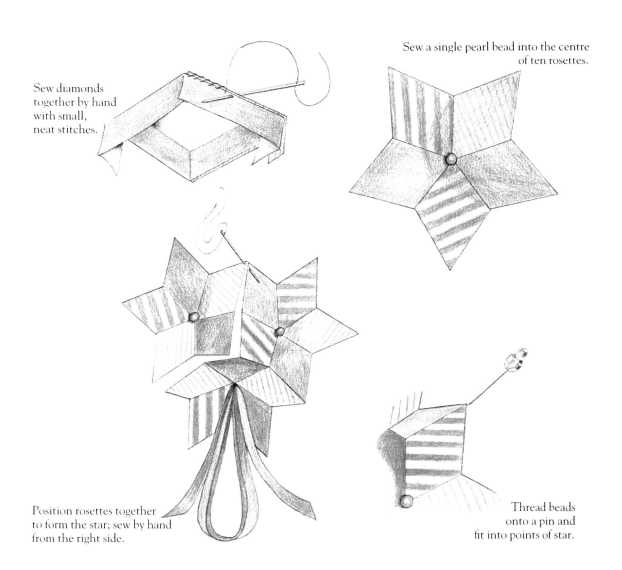

Sew diamonds together by hand with small, neat stitches.

Sew a single pearl bead into the centre of ten rosettes.

Position rosettes together to form the star; sew by hand from the right side.

Thread beads onto a pin and fit into points of star.

Festive tree

Create this pretty table tree for your party decorations. Glistening beads hang from the branches for a Christmas look but you could also use tiny artificial flowers or small glass fruits or ribbon bows.

Materials
Florists' foam cone
Thin card
2 cups of mixed paper pulp
Mixed wallpaper paste
Tissue paper
Kitchen paper roll
Acrylic paint
PVA adhesive
Silver florists' wire
Teardrop beads; small round beads

Preparation
1 Cut the card into $1\frac{1}{2}$in, $2\frac{1}{2}$in and $3\frac{1}{2}$in squares (4cm, 6cm and 9cm). Cut the squares into triangles with convex long sides.

2 Starting at the bottom, push large and medium-sized triangles into the foam tree, spacing them about $\frac{3}{4}$–$1\frac{1}{4}$in (2–3cm) apart.

3 Continue round and up the tree, working first the medium-sized triangles then the smallest at the top of the tree. Insert one small triangle at the tip.

Working the design
4 Smear a little pulp on either side of the branches to thicken them.

5 When dry, cover the tree and branches with pasted pieces of tissue. Leave to dry then apply two more layers.

Cut card squares into triangles with convex sides.

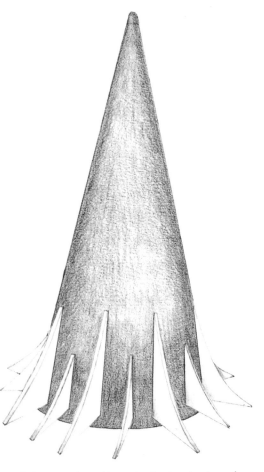

Push large and medium-sized triangles into the cone.

6 Paint the tree green. Give a final coat of diluted PVA adhesive.

7 Using a bradawl, pierce a hole in the tip of each branch. Thread a short length of wire through the hole. Thread on a bead, twist the wire ends to secure.

8 Thread small round beads on wire and join the ends to make a circlet for the top of the tree. If you prefer, a star-shaped silver bead could be stuck to the tree top.

Candlestick

This decorative candlestick is for display only and should not be used with a lighted candle. Once you have mastered the basic technique, you might attempt a branched candelabra.

Materials
Plastic-covered wire
Adhesive tape
Cardboard
Tissue paper
Mixed wallpaper paste
White emulsion paint
Gold and green paints; craft 'gems'

Preparation
1 Cut pieces of wire to 35in and 18in (89cm and 45cm) lengths. Twist the wires as shown to make the candlestick structure.

2 Cut a 2in (5cm)-diameter circle of card. Pierce a hole in the centre. Push on to the top of the candlestick stem.

3 Draw a 1in (2.5cm) diameter circle on paper. Cut a 1in (2.5cm)-wide strip of card to fit round the circle plus $\frac{1}{2}$in (1cm). Lay round the circle, overlap the ends and tape. Glue to the candlestick card circle.

4 Trace the star shape on folded paper. Open the tracing and cut 2 from card. Tape the stars to the candlestick stem, one on each side.

Working the design
5 Tear tissue into strips 4in long by $\frac{1}{4}$in wide (10cm long by 6mm wide). Paste and wrap the candlestick structure. Leave to dry.

6 Paint the candlestick with emulsion paint.

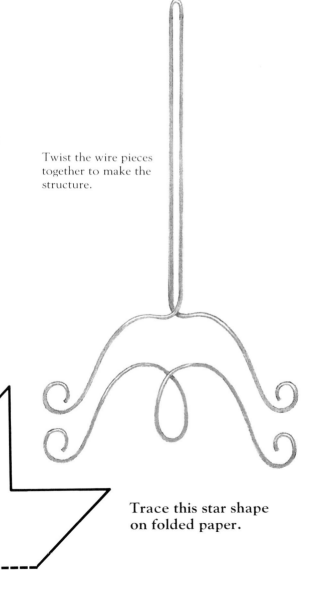

Twist the wire pieces together to make the structure.

Trace this star shape on folded paper.

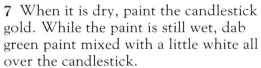
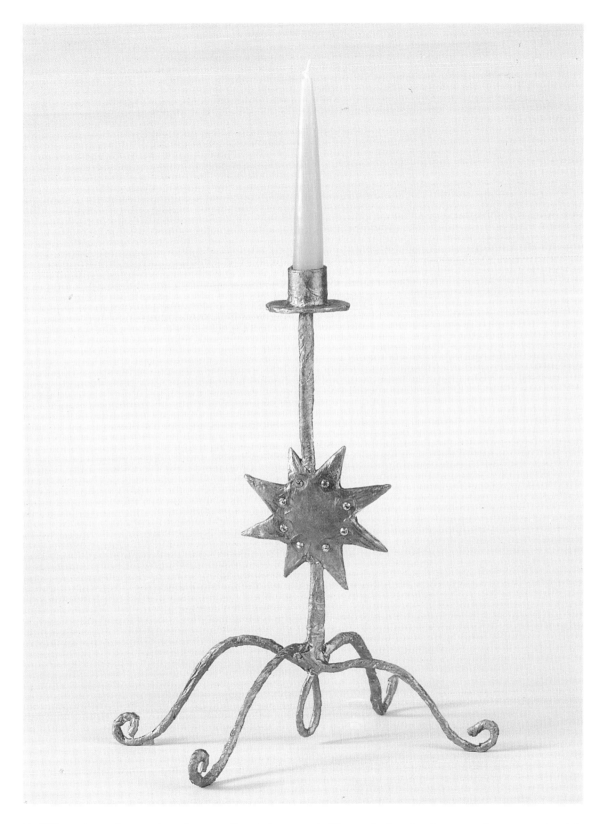

7 When it is dry, paint the candlestick gold. While the paint is still wet, dab green paint mixed with a little white all over the candlestick.

8 Pierce holes in the star shapes and stick the 'gems' in place. Clear gems have been used in the picture but coloured stones can be used if you prefer.

43

Know your place

Make your Christmas table truly memorable with these jolly Santa place markers which add a festive feeling just by being there. Simply write names on small rectangles of card and stand them in front of Santa. There's also an idea for a beautiful Christmas ring.

Materials (for 3 place markers)
Coats Anchor Mercer-Crochet cotton No. 20: 20g geranium (A) and 10g each light beige (B), black (C) and white (D); 1.25mm crochet hook; small beads (for eyes); washable polyester toy filling; small piece of card (for base).

Measurement
Approximately 5¼in (13cm) high.

Tension
First 3 rows of body measure 1in (2.5cm).

Main Section
Using A, make 52 ch, sl st to beg to form a ring.

1st round: 3 ch, 1 tr in each ch, sl st to 3rd of 3 ch.

2nd round: 3 ch, 1 tr in next tr, *1 tr in each of next 11 tr, leaving last lp of each on hook work 1 tr in each of next 2 tr, thread over and draw through all lps on hook (a joint tr is made); rep from * omitting a joint tr at end of last rep, sl st to 1st tr.

3rd round: 3 ch, 1 tr in each st, sl st to 3rd of 3 ch, 49 sts.

4th round: As 2nd rnd having 10 tr between each joint tr – 46 sts.

5th round: As 3rd rnd.

6th round: As 2nd rnd 43 sts.

7th round: 3 ch, 1 tr in each of next 11 tr, leaving last lp on hook work 1 tr in next tr, drop A, pick up B and draw through all lps on hook, fasten off A, 1 tr in back lp only of each of next 16 tr, leaving last lp on hook work 1 tr in back lp of next tr, drop B, pick up A and draw through all lps on hook, fasten off B, 1 tr in each of next 12 tr, sl st to 3rd of 3 ch.

8th and 9th rounds: As 6th rnd working into both lps of each st.

10th round: As 2nd rnd having 8 tr between each joint tr – 39 sts.

11th round: As 3rd rnd.

12th round: As 2nd rnd having 7 tr between each joint tr – 35 sts.

13th round: As 3rd rnd.

14th round: As 2nd rnd having 6 tr between each joint tr – 31 sts.

Cont in this manner until there is 1 tr between each joint tr. Fasten off leaving sufficient to thread through last row. Draw up last row and secure.

Beard
1st row: With rs facing attach D to front lp of 31st tr made on 5th rnd of main section, 1 dc in same place as join, 1 dc in front lp of each of next 17 tr, 1 ch, turn.

2nd row: Insert hook in first st and draw thread through, insert hook in next st and draw thread through, thread over and draw through all lps on hook (a joint dc made at beg of row), 1 dc in each dc to within last 2 dc, a joint dc over next 2 sts, 1 ch, turn.

Rep 2nd row until 4 sts rem.

9th row: A joint dc over first 2 sts, a joint dc over next 2 sts, 1 ch, turn.

10th row: A joint dc over next 2 dc. Fasten off.

Hat Band
Using D, make 38 ch, join with a sl st to form a ring.

1st round: 1 dc in same place as sl st, 1 dc in each ch, sl st to 1st dc.

2nd round: 3 ch, 4 tr in same place as sl st, remove lp from hook, insert hook in 3rd of 3 ch and draw dropped lp through (a starting popcorn st made, referred to as pc st), *1 ch, miss 1 dc, 5 tr in next dc, remove lp from hook, insert hook in first tr of 5 tr group

draw dropped lp through (a pc st made); rep from * ending with 1 ch, sl st to 1st pc st.
3rd round: 1 dc in same place as sl st, *1 dc in next sp, 1 dc in next pc st; rep from * ending with 1 dc in next sp, 1 sl st to 1st dc. Fasten off.

Pompon
Using D, make 2 ch.
1st round: 6 dc in 2nd ch from hook, sl st to 1st dc.
2nd and 3rd rounds: 2 dc in same place as sl st, 2 dc in each dc, 1 sl st to 1st dc.
4th round: 1 dc in same place as sl st, 1 dc in each dc, 1 sl st in 1st dc.
5th round: 1 dc in same place as sl st, *a joint dc over next 2 dc, 1 dc in next dc; rep from * omitting 1 dc at end of last rep, sl st to 1st dc.
Fasten off leaving sufficient to thread through last row. Stuff and draw up neatly.

Base
Using A, make 4 ch.
1st round: 11 tr in 4th ch from hook, sl st to 4th of 4 ch.

2nd round: 3 ch, 1 tr in same place as sl st, 2 tr in each tr, 1 sl st to 3rd of 3 ch.
3rd and 4th rounds: 3 ch, *2 tr in next tr, 1 tr in next tr; rep from * ending with 2 tr in next tr, sl st to 3rd of 3 ch.
Fasten off.

First foot
With rs facing attach C to front lp of 16 tr made on 4th rnd of base, 1 dc in same place as join, 1 dc in front lp of each of next 8 dc, 1 ch, turn.
2nd to 4th rows: As 2nd row of beard.
5th row: As 10th row of beard. Fasten off.

Second foot
With rs facing miss next 4 tr on 4th rnd of base, attach C to front lp of next tr, 1 dc in same place as join, complete as first foot.

Finishing
Stuff main section and sew pompon, hat band and beads for eyes in position. Cut a small circle of card, place to ws of base then sew base neatly in position.

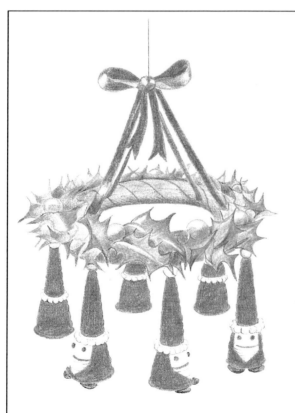

Christmas Ring
Push holly and other greenery into a florists' foam ring. Wind wide red satin ribbon over the entire ring, between the holly. Attach four narrow ribbons to the inside of the ring. Pass the ends through a brass curtain ring and knot. Tie on a large satin bow to cover the ring. Suspend the small santas, spacing them equidistantly. Glittering glass balls or other ornaments can also be added to the greenery. Thread balls on stiff wire, bend over and twist the ends, then push the wire into the foam ring. The Santa pattern is for working red dolls but they can be worked in white, green or blue to match your Christmas house decor.

Candles for Christmas Eve

These charming candlesticks are designed with little details that make them special. They can be displayed on a shelf or table or would make unusual ornaments for place settings.

Materials (for 3 large and 3 small)
2 balls (10g) Coats Anchor Mercer-Crochet Cotton No. 20 each of 469 geranium (A), white (B), 1 ball each of 623 spring green (C), 513 orange (D); 1.25mm crochet hook; washable polyester toy filling.

Measurements
Small decoration approx 3in (7.5cm) high.
Large decoration approx 3¹/₂in (9cm) high.

Tension
First 2 rows of small decoration, ⁵/₈in (15mm) in diameter.

SMALL DECORATION

Base
Using B, make 4 ch.
1st row: 15 tr in 4th ch from hook, sl st to 4th of 4 ch.
2nd row: 1 dc in same place as sl st, 1 dc in each tr, sl st to back 1p of 1st dc.
3rd row: 2 dc in same place as sl st, 2 dc in back lp only of each dc, sl st to 1st dc.
4th row: 1 dc in same place as sl st, 1 dc in each dc, sl st to first dc.
5th row: 2 dc in same place as sl st, *1 dc in next dc, 2 dc in next dc; rep from * ending with 1 dc in next dc, sl st to 1st dc.
6th row: As 4th row.
7th row: 2 dc in same place as sl st, *1 dc in each of next 2 dc, 2 dc in next dc; rep from * ending with 1 dc in each of next 2 dc, sl st to 1st dc.
8th row: As 4th row.
9th row: 2 dc in same place as sl st, *1 dc in each of next 3 dc, 2 dc in next dc; rep from * ending with 1 dc in each of next 3 dc, sl st to 1st dc.
10th row: 1 dc in same place as sl st, 1 dc in each dc, 1 sl st in front lp of 1st dc.
11th row: 1 dc in same place as sl st, 1 dc in front lp only of each dc, 1 sl st to 1st dc.

12th to 14th rows: As 4th row. Fasten off

Candle
1st row: With rs facing attach A to front lp of first dc on 2nd row of base, 3 ch, 1 tr in front lp of each dc on 2nd row of base.
2nd row: 1 tr round 3 ch made on 1st row, 1 tr round bar of each tr.
3rd row: 1 tr round bar of each tr.
Rep 3rd row 13 times more, sl st to 1st tr. Fasten off.

Top
Using A, work as base for 1 row.
2nd row: 1 dc in same place as sl st, 1 dc in each tr, 1 sl st in 1st dc. Fasten off.

Flame
Using A, make 7 ch.
1st row: 1 dc in 2nd ch from hook, 1 dc in each ch. Fasten off.
2nd row: With rs facing attach D to last dc made on 1st row, 1 dc in same place as join, cont to work along other side of foundation ch, 2 dc in first ch, 1 htr in next ch, 1 tr in next ch, 3 tr in each of next 2 ch, into next ch work 3 tr and 1 dtr, 11 ch, sl st to top of last dtr (top of flame), 3 tr in each of next 3 dc, 1 tr in next dc, 1 htr in next dc, sl st to 1st dc. Fasten off.

Handle
Using B, make 25 ch.
1st row: 1 dc in 2nd ch from hook, 1 dc in each ch, 1 ch, turn.
2nd row: 1 dc in each dc, 1 ch, turn.
3rd row: Working over previous row work 1 dc in each dc on 1st row, 1 ch, turn.
4th row: Working over previous 2 rows work 1 dc in each of first 10 dc on 1st row, 2 dc in each of next 10 dc on 1st row, 1 dc in each of next 4 dc on 1st row. Fasten off.

47

Leaf (make 2)

Using C, make 15 ch.

1st row: 1 dtr in 5th ch from hook, 3 ch, 1 dc in top of last dtr (a picot made), (into next ch work 1 dtr and 1 tr, into next ch work 1 tr and 1 dtr, a picot) 5 times, 4 ch, in same ch as last dtr work 1 sl st 4 ch and 1 dtr, a picot, cont to work along other side of foundation ch (into next ch work 1 dtr and 1 tr, into next ch work 1 tr and 1 dtr, a picot) twice, into next ch work 1 tr and 1 dtr, miss 3 ch, sl st to next ch.
Fasten off.

Flower

Using A make 2 ch.

1st row: 5 dc in 2nd ch from hook, sl st to front lp of 1st dc. Fasten off.

2nd row: Attach B to back lp of 1st dc, 3 ch, into same place as join work 3 tr 3 ch and 1 sl st, into back lp of each dc work 1 sl st 3 ch 3 tr 3 ch and 1 sl st, 1 sl st to same place as join. Fasten off.

Make one flower using A for 1st row and D for 2nd row and one flower using D for 1st row and A for 2nd row.

Make 2 more small decorations alternating colours.

Dampen and pin out to shape.

LARGE DECORATION

Base

Work as base of small decoration for 1 row.

2nd row: 1 dc in same place as sl st, 1 dc in each tr, sl st to 1st dc.

3rd row: 2 dc in same place as sl st, 2 dc in each dc, sl st to 1st dc.

4th row: 1 dc in same place as sl st, 1 dc in each dc, sl st in back lp of 1st dc.

5th row: 2 dc in same place as sl st, *working into back lp only of each dc work 1 dc in next dc, 2 dc in next dc; rep from * ending with 1 dc in next dc, 1 sl st to 1st dc.

6th to 9th rows: As 6th to 9th rows of base of small decoration.

10th row: 1 dc in same place as sl st, 1 dc in each dc, 1 sl st in 1st dc.

11th row: 2 dc in same place as sl st, *1 dc in each of next 4 dc, 2 dc in next dc; rep from * ending with 1 dc in each of next 4 dc, sl st to 1st dc.

12th and 13th rows: As 10th row.
14th to 18th rows: As 10th to 14th row of base of small decoration. Fasten off.

Candle

1st row: With rs facing attach A to front lp of first dc on 4th row of base, 3 ch, 1 tr in front lp of each ch.

2nd and 3rd rows: As 2nd and 3rd rows of candle on small decoration.
Rep 3rd row 17 times more, sl st to first tr.
Fasten off.

Top

Using A, work as base for 3 rows.
4th row: As 10th row of base. Fasten off.

Flame

Using A make 10 ch.

1st row: 1 dc in 2nd ch from hook, 1 dc in each ch.
Fasten off.

2nd row: With rs facing attach D to last dc made on 1st row, 1 dc into same place as join, cont to work along other side of foundation ch, 2 dc in first ch, 1 htr in each of next 2 ch, 1 tr in each of next 2 ch, (2 dtr in next ch) 3 times, 5 dtr in next ch, 3 ch, 1 sl st into top of last dtr (top of flame), 4 dtr in next dc, (2 dtr in next dc) 3 times, 1 tr in each of next 2 dc, 1 htr in each of next 2 dc, sl st to first dc.
Fasten off.

Handle

Using B, make 30 ch and work as handle of small decoration for 3 rows.

4th row: Working over previous 2 rows work 1 dc in each of first 13 dc on 1st row, 2 dc in each of next 12 dc on 1st row, 1 dc in each of next 4 dc on 1st row. Fasten off.
Make leaves and flowers as for small decoration.
Make 2 more large decorations alternating colours.
Dampen and pin out to shape.

Finishing

Fill candles with stuffing, sew flames to tops, then sew tops in position. Sew flowers and leaves at the base of each candle and sew handles in position as shown.

Robins on a log

The children will love to help make this chirpy choir. The robins are made from painted table tennis balls and pipe cleaners twisted into shape and glued in place.

Materials
5 table tennis balls
Red, white and brown acrylic (or poster) paints
Black pipe cleaners
2½in (6cm)-diameter cardboard tube, 12in (30cm) long
1¼in (3cm)-diameter cardboard tube, approximately 6in (15cm) long
12in (30cm) square of brown felt
8 × 12in (20 × 30cm) piece of white felt
Scraps of beige and dark green felt
Small pieces of black, orange and stiff white paper
2 small red wooden beads
All-purpose glue
Latex adhesive

Preparation
1 Using a craft knife, make a hole approximately 2in (5cm) diameter from one end of the large tube, so that the smaller tube will fit into it at an angle. Cut the end off the smaller tube at an angle to represent a sawn-off branch.

2 Pierce 2 holes in each table tennis ball, approximately ¾in (18mm) apart for inserting the legs later.

3 Use scissors to trim the fluff from 10 pipe cleaners to make them thinner.

Working the design
4 Cover both tubes with brown felt, sticking the felt down with latex adhesive. Make slits in the felt where it covers the hole in the side of the large tube and fit the smaller tube inside. If it does not fit very tightly secure in position with latex adhesive. Use a pen to mark bark lines on both tubes.

5 Cut circles of beige felt to fit over the ends of the log and branch. Mark growth circles on the felt and glue in position.

6 Cut a piece of white felt to represent snow and stick it in place on the top of the log with latex adhesive.

7 Trace the holly leaf pattern and cut 3 in green felt. Stick the leaves and red bead berries near to one end of the log.

8 Bend each pipe cleaner into legs and claws. Coat the top 1½in (4cm) with all-purpose glue and insert legs into the holes in the table tennis balls. Allow to dry.

Fit the smaller tube into the hole at an angle.

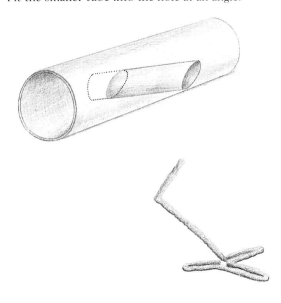

Bend the pipe cleaner to form the robin leg and claws.

9 Trace the tail shape and cut 5 from white paper. Stick the tails in place with all-purpose glue. Paint the robins (see the picture).

10 Trace the beak shape and cut 5 from orange paper. Cut 10 eyes from black paper. Fold the beaks in half. Stick the eyes and beaks in place. Paint a white highlight on each eye.

11 Use latex adhesive to fix the robins to the log.

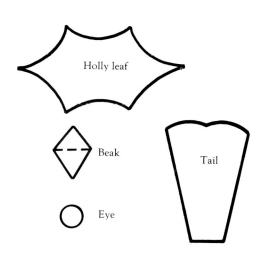

Holly leaf

Beak

Tail

Eye

Candle arrangement

This seasonal table centre is made with a pleasing variety of dried material. For a more striking effect, the finished arrangement could be sprayed gold or silver if you prefer.

Materials
8in (20cm) oval cork base
Fir cones
Poppy heads
Wheat
Sea lavender
Red broom bloom
Silver and gold spray
2in (5cm) square of florists' foam
Gold candle
Candle holder
Florists' wire
Four $2\frac{1}{2} \times 24$in (6×60cm) strips of fabric
All-purpose glue

Preparation
1 Stick the florists' foam in the centre of the cork base and allow to dry. Insert the candle holder into the centre of the foam.

2 Spread half the fir cones, half the poppy heads and half the wheat on newspaper. Spray gold and allow to dry before turning and spraying the other side.

3 In the same way, spray the other half silver.

4 Wire all the fir cones by twisting wire through them.

5 Fold the fabric strips lengthways right sides facing, stitch the long seam to make a tube. Press the seam open, turn the tube right side out and press again with the seam at the back. Fold each strip into 4 loops and twist a piece of wire around the middle.

Working the design
6 Insert pieces of sea lavender and wheat

Form the fabric tubes into 4 loops. Twist wire round the middle, then twist the ends together.

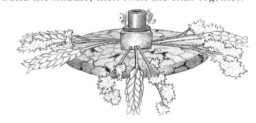

Insert wheat and sea lavender into the florists' foam to extend over the edges of the base.

Safety tip
Care should be taken with candles as the dried materials are highly inflammable. Never leave lighted candles unattended and replace them with new ones when they have burned to within about 2in (5cm) of the bottom.

into the base of the florists' foam so that they extend about 2in (5cm) over the edge of the cork base.

7 Insert the bows into the 4 corners at the base of the foam.

8 Gradually build up the shape from the bottom with sea lavender, wheat and broom bloom.

9 Insert the fir cones and poppy heads at intervals (see picture).

53

Appliquéd tablecloth

Your own embroidered festive table linens will be a talking point with friends and family. Appliqué is a simple technique and quick to do – especially when worked with a sewing machine.

Materials
36in (90cm) square of white cotton/
    polyester fabric
8in (20cm) of Christmas print fabric, 48in
    (122cm) wide
4yd (3.60m) of pre-gathered broderie
    anglaise
Fusible web

Preparation
1 Cut 1¼in (3cm)-wide strips of print fabric on the bias to make bias binding. Join these strips to make enough to go all round the cloth.

2 Trace the bow and bell shapes and make card templates. Draw round the templates on the paper side of the fusible web to make 4 bows and 8 bells. Cut out the shapes and iron on to the back of the Christmas print fabric. Cut out.

Working the design
3 Round off the corners of the white cotton square. Cut out. Position two bells and a bow in each corner, remove the paper backing and iron in place. Stitch around the shapes using a close zig-zag machine-stitch.

Trace these shapes for the bell and bow appliqué.

Finishing
4 Fold the bias strip lengthways with wrong sides facing and press lightly. Open out and press the edges to meet at the centre crease.

5 Apply the bias binding round the edges of the cloth.

6 Baste and then stitch or sew the broderie anglaise to the wrong side of the cloth, so that the lacy edge shows on the right side.

Seasonal design

Invite friends for an informal buffet supper over the Christmas season and present the food on a bright buffet cloth embroidered with holly leaves and berries.

Materials

Two pieces of white evenweave cotton
 fabric, 32 × 2½in (81 × 6cm), 28–30
 threads to 1in (2.5cm)
Piece of Christmas-print cotton fabric,
 44 × 32in (112 × 81cm)
Anchor stranded cottons as follows: four
skeins of 228 green, one skein of 47 red.

Working the embroidery

1 Using all six strands of embroidery cotton
together, work the holly design along the
centre of each length of white fabric. Work
cross stitches across four threads.

2 Cut a strip off each end of the Christmas
print fabric, 4½in (11.5cm) from the
selvedge.

3 Insert the embroidered strips between the
two pieces of Christmas fabric. Work a
double line of top stitching on both edges.
Trim off the excess white fabric on the
wrong side.

4 Turn under and stitch a hem on the long
edges. Use a contrasting thread if you like.

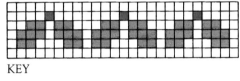

KEY

■ 47
□ 228

Work the holly and berry motif on a strip of hessian and
stitch to the edges of a felt Christmas tree cloth for a
seasonal decoration

Holiday tablecloth

A festive Christmas table starts with the cloth and this parcel design has plenty of surprises in store with the elasticated pockets which make super hidey-holes for little gifts.

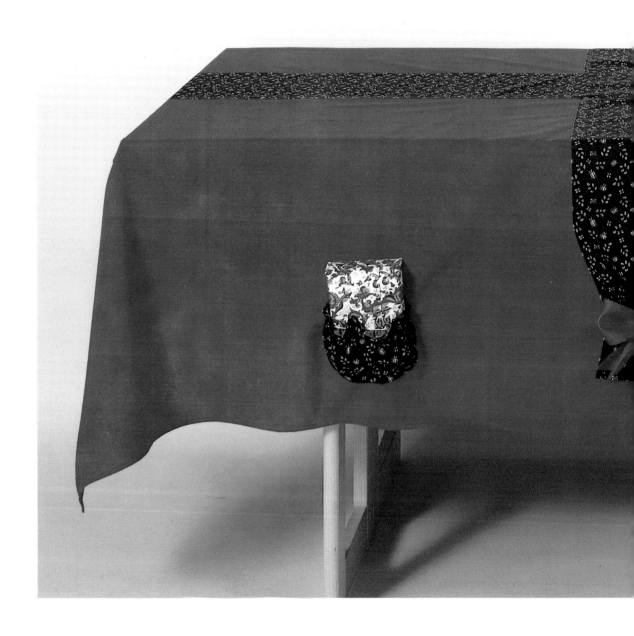

Materials

To fit 57 × 35in (145 × 89cm) table
2yd (1.90m) of red sheeting 90in (228cm) wide
1¼yd (1.50m) of 36in (90cm) wide green printed cotton
3½yd (3.20m) of 3in (8cm) wide satin ribbon
1⅜yd (1.20m) of ⅛in (3mm) wide elastic

Making the tablecloth

1 Hem around the red sheeting, turning raw edge under ¼in (6mm) twice and machine-stitching. Mitre each corner.

2 Using the green printed cotton, cut 2 parcel strips 44 × 10in (112 × 25cm) and stitch together to form one long strip of 88in (224cm). Cut a further 2 strips

33 × 10in (84 × 25cm) and again, stitch them together to form one long strip 66in (168cm).

3 Neaten the sides of each strip by turning raw edge under ½in (1cm). Turn each end under twice, to completely encase the raw edges. Machine-stitch across the end and approx 4¼in (11cm) up each side. Then gather-stitch across each end of both strips approx 4in (10cm) from the hem, and pull up so that the gathered material is 5½in (14cm) wide.

4 Position the parcel ties on the red cloth, crossing them at the centre. Machine-stitch down the side edges of both strips stopping at the gathered-stitching and thus leaving the remaining

ends free. Cut the ribbon into 4 equal lengths, tie each one into a bow and add a large red bow at the gathered end of each parcel strip.

5 To make the surprise pockets fold the patterned fabric in half lengthways and cut 8 pocket shapes using the pattern. Hem the top edge and then turn under and press ½in (1cm) on the remaining edges. Cut a 6in (15cm) length of elastic for each pocket and stitch to the wrong side of the pocket, 1in (2.5cm) from the top hem, stretching the elastic to full width as you go.

6 Finally top stitch a pocket either side of the parcel strips, placing them level with the ribbon bows.

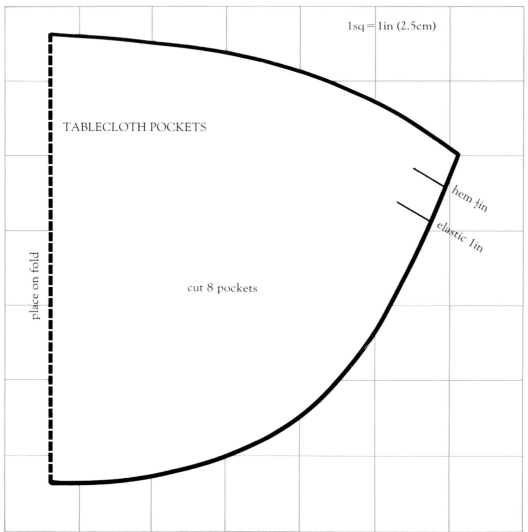

1sq = 1in (2.5cm)

TABLECLOTH POCKETS

place on fold

cut 8 pockets

hem ½in

elastic 1in

NAPKIN FOLDING

Decoratively folded serviettes and table napkins add a special finish to party tables and buffets. Good effects can be achieved with just a few simple folds.

Triangle: Fold the fabric into four then in half diagonally.

Roll: Fold the fabric into four, roll it loosely. Tie a ribbon round the middle, or use a plain ring decorated with a few dried flowers or a sprig of silk mistletoe.

Candle: Fold the fabric in half diagonally, roll it up tightly from the fold. Fold in half again, bringing the ends up and insert into a wine glass.

Heart: Fold the fabric in half then into thirds.

Fan: Fold the fabric concertina-fashion. Fold in half and insert the folded edge into a wine glass, spreading the fan over the rim of the glass.

Fan: Fold the napkin concertina-fashion.

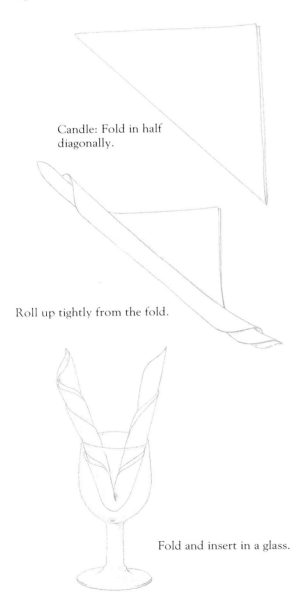

Candle: Fold in half diagonally.

Roll up tightly from the fold.

Fold and insert in a glass.

Spread the fan over the glass rim.

To make fabric serviettes or napkins, cut plain or patterned fabric into 14 or 16in (35 or 40cm) squares. Work wide, close satin stitch all round the square, about $\frac{1}{2}$in (12mm) from the edge and then trim the excess fabric away after stitching. Coarsely-woven fabrics, such as polyester linen, could be frayed back to make a fringe. Machine stitch all round with an open zigzag stitch about $\frac{1}{2}$in (12mm) from the edge. Snip into the edges all round at 2in (5cm) intervals, then pull out the fabric threads, up to the line of stitching.

Surprises in store

These cone boxes are ideal for jewellery and other small special gifts. Folded to shape from one piece of card, they are quick to make and a pleasure to decorate with colourful scraps and trims.

Materials
Thin card
Giftwrap paper
Spray adhesive
Clear craft glue
Victorian paper scraps or other trims
Cord for loops
Small wad punch

Making the boxes
1 Trace the full-sized pattern on pages 76–77, joining lines where indicated with arrows. Trace shape on to card. Cut around the outline and crease along the fold lines. Bend the cone into shape.

2 Flatten the shape, and spray the right side with adhesive. Press on to giftwrap paper, smooth flat and cut round the card edges. Pierce a hole through the centre of the lid. Re-crease along the fold lines to shape the box.

3 Spread adhesive along the side flap and press to stick. Thread a loop of cord through the hole in the lid and knot on the underside. Stick a decorative scrap or trim on the box front.

4 To fasten the lid closed, stick a little double-sided sticky tape on the right side of the lid flaps. Remove the protective paper when the gift is inside, and seal by placing the flaps inside the box.

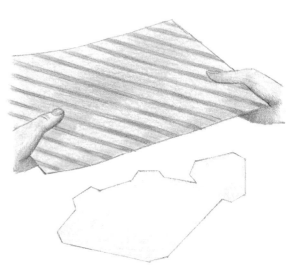

Spray the card with adhesive, press on a piece of gift paper

Glue the side flap and form the cone. Knot a cord loop through the lid hole

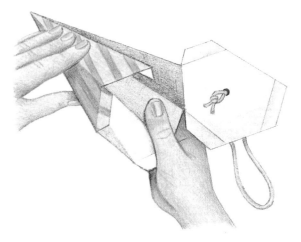

Make the boxes in seasonal colours to hang as decorations or special favours on the Christmas tree. Decorate the fronts with baubles or scraps of winter greenery and berries and fill with sweets, nuts or candied fruits.

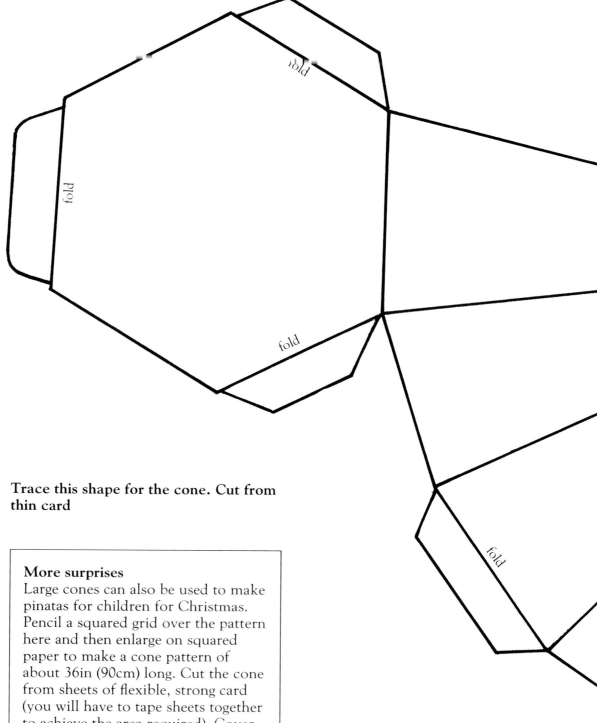

fold

fold

fold

fold

**Trace this shape for the cone. Cut from
thin card**

More surprises

Large cones can also be used to make
pinatas for children for Christmas.
Pencil a squared grid over the pattern
here and then enlarge on squared
paper to make a cone pattern of
about 36in (90cm) long. Cut the cone
from sheets of flexible, strong card
(you will have to tape sheets together
to achieve the area required). Cover
the card with bright Christmas paper
or paint Christmas designs over it.
Fill the cone with small gifts and
hang it high on the wall or over a
doorway. During the party, children
are given thin sticks and encouraged
to beat the pinata until it opens and
showers them with gifts.

Table gifts
Why not make the cone boxes in
gold or silver card for special table
decorations. Stuff the cones with
coloured tissue and tuck a small gift
inside. Tie ribbons to the top of the
cone with two or three Christmas
baubles and perhaps a small sprig of
fir. Heap the cones in the middle of
the party table, with a single ribbon
leading from each cone to a guest. At
the end of the party, guests pull a
cone towards them.

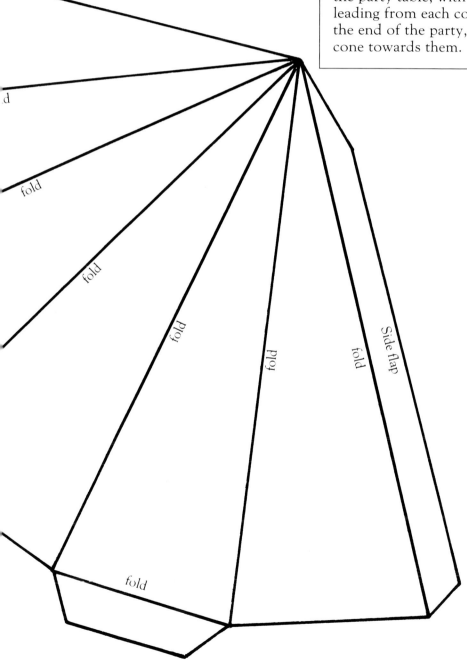

d

fold

fold

fold

fold

fold

Side flap

fold

Special greetings

Both designs, the bells and the festive tree, use the misty effect of a top layer of organza to soften the strong colour of the felt beneath.

CHRISTMAS TREE
Materials
Green felt 3³/₄in (9.5cm) square
Pale green organza 3³/₄in (9.5cm) square
Twilleys Goldfingering crochet thread (or
   thick metallic embroidery thread)
13 gold beads ¹/₈in (3mm) diameter
Spray mount glue (or general purpose glue)
Card with pre-cut window, to take finished
   image 3³/₄in (9.5cm).

Preparation
1 Trace the tree shape and transfer onto
thin card. Cut out and use as a template to
cut the shape from green felt.

2 Spray glue on the shape and place onto
the middle of the pale green organza.

3 Place the organza down with the green
felt shape underneath and transfer the lines
for the gold stitching onto the top of the
organza.

Working the embroidery
4 Work backstitch on the lines with the
gold thread. Make a double cross stitch at
the top of the tree for the star. Work straight
stitches across for the tub.

5 Sew on the gold beads.

6 Spread glue round the window of the
card on the inside and place the
embroidery in position. Press firmly and
leave to dry, then glue the return fold
around the embroidery and press firmly.

Materials needed (for the bells)

Fuschia pink felt 3³/₄in (9.5cm) square
Pale pink organza 3³/₄in (9.5cm) square
Silver thread Mez Ophir No 0301
Small length of white parcel ribbon
1 small glass bead
Pre-cut card with a window to take work
 3³/₄in (9.5cm).

Preparation

1 Trace the bells' shape and transfer to thin card. Cut out and use as a template to cut the shape from pink felt. Spray glue on the shape and place down onto the middle of the pink organza. Leave to dry.

2 Turn the organza over and transfer the pattern lines of the bells onto it.

Working the embroidery

3 Work backstitch neatly on the lines of the bells, leaving the lower edges of the main bell until last. Use a neat, close, chain stitch to embroider this line. Work small straight stitches for the clapper and sew the glass bead at the bottom.

Making up

Follow the instructions for the first card. The reversed shadow effect using organza can be utilized to make many different cards from these two designs. You could also use chiffon or voile as the top layer. Try different combinations using other coloured felts underneath.

> These motifs are ideal for making soft Christmas tree decorations. Cut the shapes from doubled felt and embroider the design lines, adding beads and sequins. Sew the two shapes together, stuffing them lightly with polyester wadding. Attach a gold thread hanger.

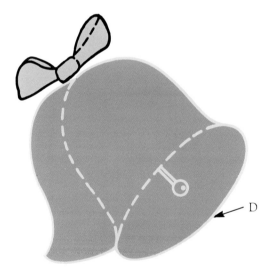

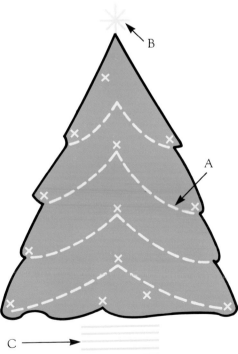

KEY
A – Backstitch
B – Double cross stitch
C – Straight stitch
D – Chain stitch

Season's greetings

Make an extra-special Christmas card by embroidering your own; these three designs are very simple. For variety, work the designs on different-coloured backgrounds; the snowflake, for instance, would look effective on rich green or midnight blue.

Materials

Candy stick card
Piece of pale green Aida fabric, 5 × 4in
(13 × 10cm), 11 threads to 1in (2.5cm)
Anchor stranded cottons as follows: one
skein each of 46 red, 230 green, 01
white
White oval-window card blank.

Christmas tree card
Piece of white Aida fabric, 5 × 4in
(13 × 10cm), 11 threads to
1in (2.5cm)
Anchor stranded cottons as follows: one
skein each of 244 green, 291 yellow,
46 red, 89 pink
Red rectangular-window card blank.

Season's greetings

Snowflake card
Piece of red Aida fabric, 4in (10cm) square,
    14 threads to 1in (2.5cm)
Anchor stranded cotton as follows: one
    skein of 01 white
White round-window card blank.

Preparation
1 Measure and mark the middle of the
fabric with lines of basting stitches,
vertically and horizontally.

Working the embroidery
2 On all three charts, the middle of the
design is indicated with arrows on the edges.
This corresponds with the marked middle of
the fabric. Using all six strands of thread for
the candy stick and Christmas tree, and
three strands for the snowflake, work the
designs following the charts and keys.

Finishing
3 Press the finished embroidery on the
wrong side with a warm iron.

4 Spread glue around the edges of the
window on the inside of the card blank, and
position the embroidery behind the window.

5 On the inside of the card, cover the left-
hand flap with a layer of glue and fold it over
to enclose the embroidery. Leave to dry.

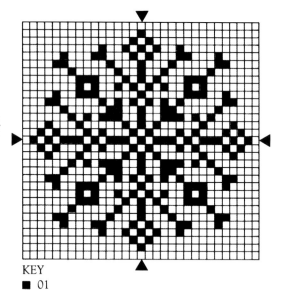

KEY
■ 01

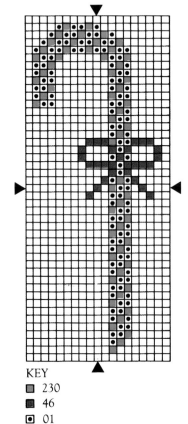

KEY
▨ 230
■ 46
◉ 01

KEY
▨ 244   ▨ 89
■ 46   □ 291

Santa Claus stocking

Hang this colourful Christmas stocking above the mantelpiece ready for Santa Claus to fill it with lots of surprises. The full boot shape ensures plenty of room to pack in presents.

Materials

To make 2 stockings:
20in (50cm) of 36in (90cm) wide red felt
White and green felt squares
Black fabric paint
Oddment of orange felt
DK wool oddments and polyester
    stuffing
1yd (90cm) of 1in (2.5cm) wide satin ribbon
Decorative fluffy balls and sequins
Fabric adhesive

Making the stockings

1 Fold the ends of the felt to meet in the middle and using the graph pattern cut 2 stocking pieces for each stocking. For the snowman, fold a square of white felt in half and placing the pattern against the fold, cut one body and head piece. Cut holly from green felt.

2 Using the fabric paint, paint the coal black eyes and mouth on the face and leaf detail on the holly. Alternatively, embroider French knot eyes and use a running stitch for the mouth. Next, cut a triangle of orange felt for the carrot nose. Fold in half and stitch two sides together, lightly stuff and hand sew to the face.

3 Whilst the paint dries, knit the woolly hat and scarf. For the hat, cast on 10 stitches of DK yarn. Knit two rows, working in stocking stitch (stockinet stitch). Decrease at each end of the next and alternate rows until one stitch remains. Cast off. For the scarf, cast on 4 stitches and garter-stitch for 10 rows. Change colour if desired and knit another 10 rows. Change to a third colour for the next 20 rows, then repeat colours one and two for another 10 rows each. Add a ½in (1cm) fringe to each end.

4 Wrap the scarf around the snowman's neck and then pin him to one boot section approximately in the centre. Machine-stitch around the edges, stopping either side of the scarf and leaving an opening at the top. Stuff lightly, pushing the stuffing through the neck and rounding out his tummy. Slipstitch the opening and then hand sew the woolly hat at a jaunty angle.

5 Finish the snowman with a pompon for his hat and fluffy balls for his tummy held firmly in place by fabric adhesive paint/glue. Add a group of white fluffy snowballs, attached with adhesive.

6 Position the holly leaves as desired on the boot and hand sew in place. Add groups of red sequin berries.

7 Fold the top of both boot sections under 1in (2.5cm) and stitch in place. Cut a 9in (23cm) length of satin ribbon for the hanging loop. Then pin the back to the front boot section with wrong sides together, pinning the ribbon loop in the seam allowance at the top edge. Using a contrasting coloured thread, machine-stitch around the boot edges, allowing ½in (1cm) seam allowance. Trim to ¼in (6mm) from the stitching.

8 Tie the remaining ribbon into a decorative bow for the top of the boot. Catch stitch in place at the centre front.

Trace offs for leaf templates

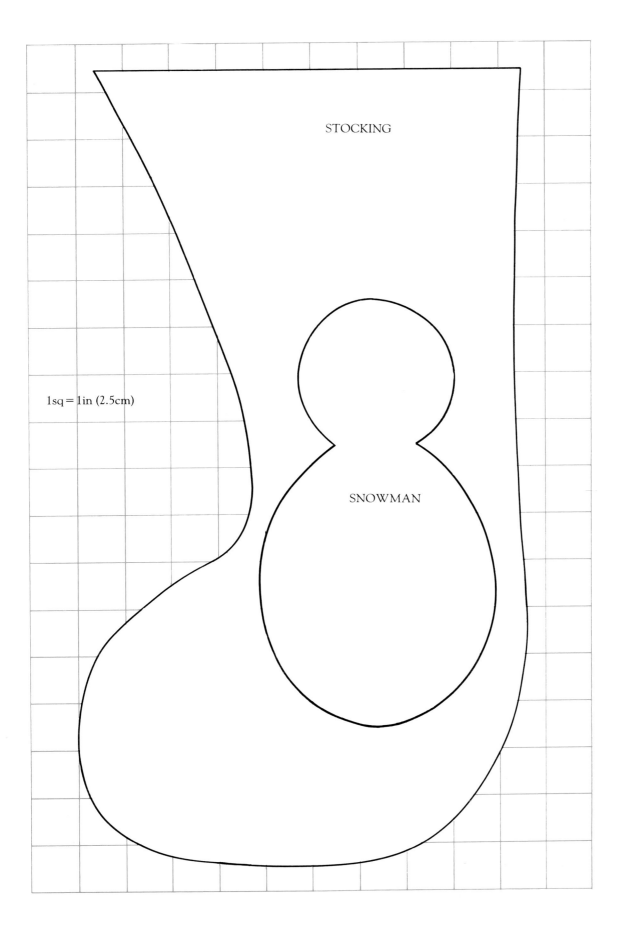

STOCKING

SNOWMAN

1sq = 1in (2.5cm)

Carried away

A tote bag is an ever popular, versatile container – the ideal solution for wrapping an awkwardly shaped gift, and attractive enough to keep as a lightweight holdall for all kinds of miscellaneous materials.

Materials

Decorative giftwrap paper (or patterned wallpaper)
Cartridge paper (or wall lining paper)
Thin card
Spray adhesive
Stick adhesive
Cord or ribbon for handles
String for gift tags
Hole punch

Making tote bags

A tote bag can be any size you wish to make, simply by adapting the basic pattern and following one basic rule: the depth of the base overlap sections on the bag (marked on pattern **A** plus half again) should always measure more than half the depth (marked **A**) of each tote side. All **A** measurements should be equal, so that the bag holds its shape well and folds flat. By simply checking these proportions you can make professional looking tote bags, from mini totes to maxi sizes. When making large bags, join papers at each side so that the joins do not show.

Making the lining

1 Following the diagram (on page 76) draw the tote measurements onto a sheet of cartridge (or a similar weight of paper). Cut out. Starting with the main vertical lines, crease the fold lines to shape. Crease the base line and the fold line which runs across the back section. Carefully crease the side triangular shaped sections. Next, fold the side lines together, and pinch the triangles into place. Open out again.

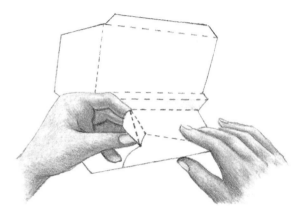

Spread glue along the right side of the side flap, press to the inside edge of the tote side

With one hand inside as a support, press the flaps together to stick

Press the base section along the crease lines

Covering the lining

2 Lay the cartridge paper flat, creased side facing and spray with adhesive. Lay the covering paper flat wrong side facing, and press the cartridge, sticky side down, on to this. Position it so that there is an overlap of covering paper at the top edge of about 3in (7.5cm). Smooth flat on both sides of paper. Trim level with the cartridge edges, adjusting the top overlap size accurately if necessary. Fold along the creases to shape the paper smoothly.

3 Cut a reinforcing strip of thin card to the same depth as the overlap and as wide as the tote (excluding the side flap) and stick across the top of the cartridge paper. Spread adhesive underneath the top overlap and press flat to stick to the card strip.

4 Spread adhesive along the right side of the side flap, and press to the inside edge of the tote side. Align the edges, and top and base lines neatly. Press to stick.

5 Turn the bag upside down. Spread adhesive on the edges of the right sides of the base side flaps, and along the edge of the wrong side of the under flap. With one hand inside the bag as support, press the flaps together to stick, making sure that the bag keeps its shape. Now spread adhesive under the remaining base flap, and press to stick.

6 Smooth the tote bag edges, making sure that they are all aligned. Gently press the base section flat along the crease lines, so that the base rests flat against the bag.

The handles

7 Position the handles to suit the proportions of the bag. The holes for the handles are marked with a hole punch. To achieve a good balance, position these between a third to a quarter of the front width in from each side. Place the holes about ¾in (18mm) down from the top edge, or as far as the punch will reach, to avoid tearing the paper.

Diagram for the tote bag

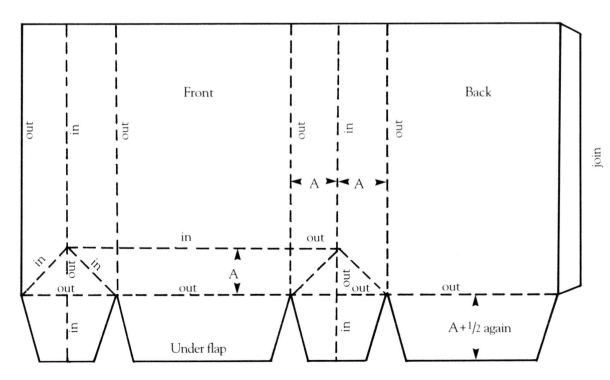

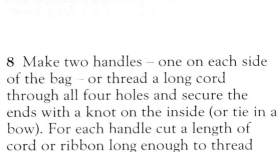

8 Make two handles – one on each side of the bag – or thread a long cord through all four holes and secure the ends with a knot on the inside (or tie in a bow). For each handle cut a length of cord or ribbon long enough to thread through both holes and provide a comfortable handle.

Gift tags

9 Make a gift tag to match or contrast with the tote bag. Laminate a piece of giftwrap to cartridge paper or thin card, and crease to mark a centre fold. Cut round to the shape required, and punch a hole near the fold to hold the tie. Alternatively, cut round the outline of a suitable motif and laminate this to paper or card.

Happy Christmas

Almost everyone loves a stocking that they can hang up at Christmas. The anticipation and excitement of prettily wrapped little gifts is all part of the joy. This festive-looking stocking will be treasured from year to year – and becomes part of the house decorations as well.

Materials
Red Christmas print fabric, 36 × 24in (90 × 60cm)
Green and white Christmas print fabric, 20 × 8in (50 × 20cm), for the cuff
Lightweight polyester wadding, 36 × 30in (90 × 76cm)
Green and red felt, 6in (15cm) squares
Gold Lurex ribbon, ⅛in (3mm) wide, 6¾yd (6.20m)
Double-edged lace, 1in (2.5cm) wide, 40in (1m)
Gold-edge white satin ribbon, ⅜in (9mm) wide, 40in (1m)
Green satin ribbon, ⅛in (3mm) wide, 2½yd (2.30m)

Preparation
1 On squared paper, draw the pattern from the graph pattern (scale: 1 sq = 1in (2.5cm). Use the pattern to cut 4 stocking shapes from the red Christmas fabric (2 for the lining). Cut 2 stockings from wadding.

Making the stocking
2 Match the wadding pieces to the wrong side of the two main stocking pieces. Baste together. Pin the narrow gold ribbon in a lattice pattern over one stocking front, forming 2in (5cm) squares. Tie green ribbon bows and sew one to each intersection, catching the crossed ribbons together.

3 Baste the stocking back to the front, right sides facing. Stitch all round, leaving the top open.

4 Baste and stitch the 2 lining stockings together, leaving a 6in (15cm) opening in one side seam.

5 From red fabric, cut a loop piece 8 × 1½in (20 × 4cm). Fold in half lengthways right sides facing and stitch, taking a ¼in (6mm) seam. Turn to the right side. Press. Fold and stitch to the top edge at the back of the main stocking.

6 Cut a piece of wadding half the depth of the green fabric cuff piece. Baste the wadding to the upper half of the cuff on the wrong side. Pin lace over the wadded part of the cuff, ¾in (18mm) from the top edge and again across the centre. Pin and stitch the gold and white ribbon centrally over the lace, anchoring it in place. Baste and then stitch the cuff into a ring. Fold in half, matching the raw edges, and baste to the top of main stocking.

7 Place the lining over the main stockings, right sides facing. Baste then stitch round the top edges, catching in the loop and cuff. Turn through the opening in the lining. Slipstitch the opening closed. Push the lining down inside the stocking.

8 **Decoration:** Trace the holly leaf and berry patterns. From green felt cut 6 leaves. Pin and baste together in pairs. Stitch all round, adding a small amount of wadding as you sew. Trim the seam allowance closely.

9 From red felt cut 2 berries. Work a gathering thread round the outer edges and pull up tightly round a small amount of wadding to form the berry. Fasten off the thread end. Stitch the leaves and berries to the cuff.

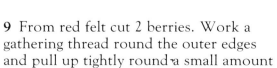

Trace the holly leaves and berry patterns

Bags of money
The Christmas stocking pattern can be adapted to make a charming and unusual advent decoration. Have the pattern reduced photographically so that the stocking is about 4in (10cm) long. Cut the shape from coloured felt (2 pieces for each stocking) using pinking shears so that a decorative edge is obtained. Sew two shapes together. On one side brush numbers 1–24 in clear glue and, before it dries, sprinkle glitter dust on the glue. If you like, the other side of the felt stockings can have a Christmas message spelled out in glitter dust letters, such as UNTO US A CHILD IS BORN, with a star on the last stocking. Make felt hangers for each stocking, sewing them into the back edge. Small sweets or candies can be placed inside or you might decide to make gifts of coins. Hang the stockings along a length of ribbon for a wall decoration, or fasten them to the overmantle. Alternatively, they could be hung on the Christmas tree.

Deck with holly
The trace-off holly leaves can be used for all kinds of Christmas fun. Cut them from card and use them as templates to cut shapes from green-coloured fondant icing for cakes. Use the shapes for making your own Christmas cards or for making leaf-shaped gift tags. Cut holly leaf templates from thin card and stencil red and green leaves on to white kitchen paper for an inexpensive giftwrap. Make a potato printing block by cutting a leaf shape into the cut surface and show children how to print holly leaves on to cards and invitations.

Christmas Stocking

Draw the pattern for the stocking on squared paper, scale 1 sq = 1in (2.5cm)

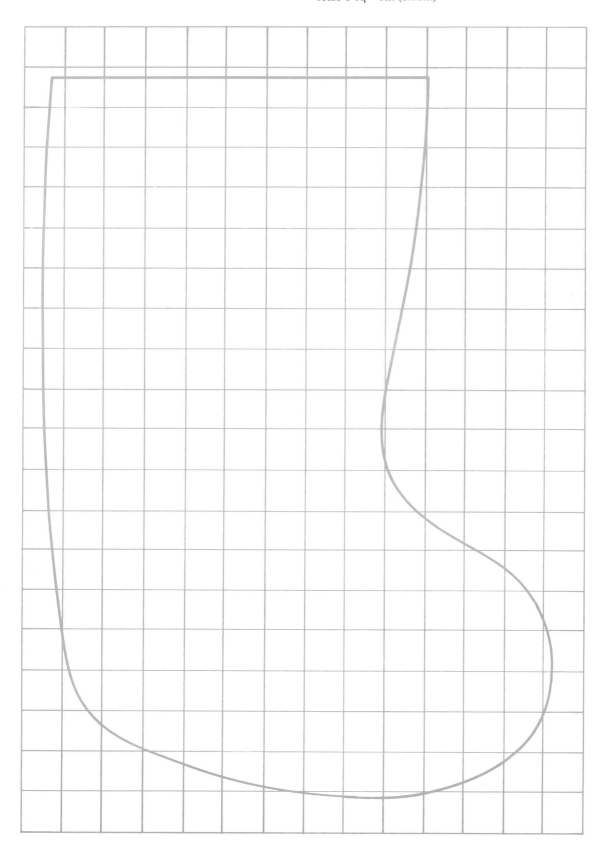

Christmas box

A storage box for jewellery or keepsakes can be created from any plain cardboard box using newspaper layering. This box has been decorated with holly leaves and berries for a festive look.

Materials
Cardboard box with lid
Newspaper torn into small strips
Kitchen paper roll
Mixed wallpaper paste
Tissue paper
Scraps of thin cardboard
Small beads
PVA adhesive
White emulsion paint
Acrylic paints; gold paint

Preparation
1 Set the lid on the box and pencil round the edges of the lid.

Working the design
2 Paste newspaper strips round the sides of the box up to the pencilled line and on the bottom, overlapping the strips. Leave to dry.

3 Apply strips to the outside of the lid but do not wrap the strips over to the inside or the lid will not fit on the box later. Leave to dry.

4 Work the box again, this time with strips of kitchen paper. Leave to dry and work 7 layers in all, alternating between newspaper and kitchen paper.

5 In the same way, work a total of 4 layers on the lid.

6 Finish both the box and the lid with tissue strips to give a smooth finish to the surface and the edges.

7 Try the lid on the box. It should go on easily and the papered surfaces should line up.

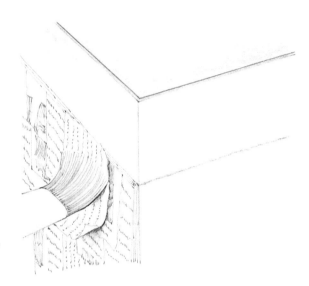

Apply newspaper strips only to the pencilled line.

Decoration
8 Cut holly leaves from thin card. Stick in place on the lid with the berries, using PVA adhesive.

9 When dry, paste tissue paper over the leaves and berries, brushing the tissue into place so that the decoration shows through clearly.

10 Paint the whole box with 2 coats of white emulsion paint.

11 Finish the box and decoration with acrylic paints and gold paint.

Heaven scent

Filled with lavender or pot-pourri, these pretty pomanders make attractive gifts to hang in the wardrobe or slip between clothes in a drawer. The pomanders are made from pentagon-shaped patches, all cut from the same fabric.

Materials
Pentagon template with 1in (2.5cm) sides
Pieces of pretty cotton fabrics
Matching threads
Ribbon
Pot-pourri or lavender

Preparation
1 Use the template to cut 12 paper pentagons. Cut the same number of fabric pentagons, adding ⅛in (6mm) all round.

2 Pin a paper centrally on each fabric pentagon, fold over the fabric edges and baste to secure.

Making a pomander
3 Take one pentagon as the base and oversew a pentagon to each side of the five sides (see illustration). Press the patchwork.

4 Oversew all the adjacent sides together. Work the other half of the pomander in the same way. Snip the basting threads and shake out the papers.

5 With right sides facing, sew the two halves together, leaving a gap for filling.

Finishing
6 Turn through and fill the pomander with pot-pourri or lavender. Insert a ribbon loop and slipstitch to close the gap.

More ideas for pentagon balls
To make Christmas tree baubles, use card instead of paper and leave the card in place after sewing up is completed. The last seam will have to be done from the right side. Use shiny and glittering fabrics, sew on gold or silver braids along the seams. Trim the balls with beads and sequins.

Soft baby balls
Draw round the pentagon template to enlarge the size. Cut shapes from soft, washable fabrics and sew together to make stuffed toy balls for babies.

A bell can be pushed into the ball while stuffing. Make sure all seams are securely finished off to prevent them from opening and stuffing seeping out.

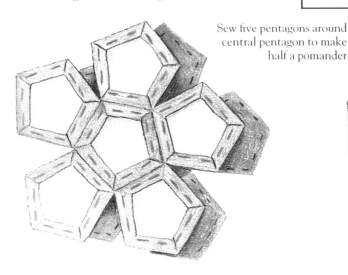

Sew five pentagons around central pentagon to make half a pomander

Sew two half pomanders together, leaving 2 sides open for filling.

Reindeer

This Christmas reindeer toy is straight from Lapland. His name is, of course, Rudolf – you can tell by his red nose!

Materials
1 (50g) ball Sirdar Country Style Double Knitting in beige, small quantity in black, brown and red; oddments of yarn for embroidery; pair of 4mm/No 8 knitting needles; washable polyester toy filling.
Measurement
Approx 12in (30cm) tall.
Tension
24 sts and 30 rows to 4in (10cm) measured over st st on 4mm/No 8 needles.

Body (make 1)
Using beige, cast on 5 sts.
* Working in st st, work as follows:
Next row (wrong side): P.
Next row: Inc knitwise in every st * – 10 sts.
Rep from * to * until there are 80 sts.
Work a further 7in (18cm) straight, ending p row.
** **Next row:** (K2 tog) to end.
Next row: P ** – 40 sts.
Rep from ** to ** until 5 sts rem.
Run a thread through rem sts.

Head (make 1)
Using brown, cast on 5 sts.
Work as given for body from * to * until there are 40 sts.
Work 7 rows straight.
Change to beige and work a further 20 rows, so ending p row.
Work as given for body from ** to ** until 5 sts rem.
Run a thread through rem sts.

Neck (make 1)
Using beige, cast on 36 sts.
Beg k row, work 14 rows in st st.
Cast off loosely.

Legs (make 4)
Using beige, cast on 20 sts.

Beg k row and working in st st, work 18 rows.
Change to brown and work 6 rows.
Change to black and work 2 rows, then work as given for body from ** to ** until 5 sts rem.
Run a thread through rem sts.

Tail (make 1)
Using brown, cast on 8 sts.
Beg k row and working in st st, dec 1 st each end of every 3rd row until 2 sts rem.
Change to beige and inc 1 st each end of next, then every 3rd row until there are 8 sts.
Work 2 rows.
Cast off.

Ears (make 2)
Using beige, cast on 10 sts.
Beg k row and working in st st, work 8 rows.
Dec 1 st each end of next 2 rows – 6 sts.
Change to brown and inc 1 st each end of next 2 rows – 10 sts.
Work 8 rows.
Cast off.

Nose (make 1)
Using red, cast on 6 sts and work as given for body from * to * once – 12 sts.
Work 7 rows straight.
Next row: (K2 tog) to end – 6 sts.
Run a thread through rem sts.

Antler stems (make 2)
Using brown, cast on 10 sts.
Beg k row and working in st st, work 16 rows straight, ending p row.
Next row: (K2 tog) to end – 5 sts.
Run a thread through rem sts.

Antler lower branches (make 2)
Using brown, work as for antler stems, but work only 10 rows straight.

Antler upper branches (make 2)

Using brown, work as for antler stems, but work only 6 rows straight.

Finishing

Join body seam leaving an opening, fill, close opening. Join leg seams matching colours, fill and attach with ends flat. Join side edges of neck to form a cylinder and attach to body by cast on edge, fill neck. Join head seam matching colours, fill before completing seam and attach to top of neck with brown end towards the front. Fill and attach nose. Double ears, join edges and attach with bases doubled. Seam and fill antler branches and stems. Attach stems to head and branches to stems. Double tail, seam and attach. Embroider features (see picture).

Snowman

This snowman is very easy to make, for a toy, a Christmas decoration or for a table centre for a child's party. Adapt the colours of the scarf and hat to suit your own ideas.

Materials
1 (50g) ball Sirdar Country Style Double Knitting in white; small quantities of Double Knitting in royal blue, black, yellow and orange; pair each 3¾mm/No 9 and 4mm/ No 8 knitting needles; washable polyester toy filling.

Measurement
Approx 12in (30cm) tall.

Tension
24 sts and 30 rows to 4in (10cm) measured over st st on 4mm/No 8 needles.

Main piece (make 1)
Using 4mm needles and white, cast on 9 sts.
* Working in st st, work as follows:
Next row (wrong side): P.
Next row: Inc knitwise in every st * – 18 sts.
Rep the last 2 rows until there are 72 sts.
Work 8in (20cm) straight, ending p row.
** **Next row:** (K2 tog) to end.
Next row: P ** – 36 sts.
Rep the last 2 rows until 9 sts rem. Run a thread through rem sts.

Head (make 1)
Using 4mm needles and white, cast on 6 sts.
Work as given for main piece from * to * until there are 48 sts.
Work 3in (8cm) straight, ending p row.
Work as given for main piece from ** to ** until 6 sts rem.
Run a thread through rem sts.

Hat
Using 3¾mm needles and blue, cast on 48 sts.
Work 4 rows in k1, p1 rib.
Change to 4mm needles. Beg k row and working in st st, work 2 rows.
Change to yellow and work 4 rows.

Change to blue and work 2 rows, so ending p row.
Work as given for main piece from ** to ** until 6 sts rem. Run a thread through rem sts.

Scarf
Using 3¾mm needles and blue, cast on 13 sts.
Rib row 1: K2, (p1, k1) to last st, k1.
Rib row 2: K1, (p1, k1) to end.
Rep these 2 rows 3 more times.
*** Change to yellow and k 1 row.
Beg rib row 2, work 3 rows in rib.
Change to blue and k 1 row ***.
Beg rib row 2, cont in rib until scarf measures 16in (41cm) from cast on edge, ending rib row 2.
Rep from *** to ***.
Beg rib row 2, work 7 rows in rib.
Cast off in rib.

Pieces of coal (make 5)
Using 4mm needles and black, cast on 1 st and k 3 times into st.
Next row: P.
Next row: K.
P3 tog, fasten off.

Carrot for nose
Using 4mm needles and orange, cast on 9 sts.
Beg k row and working in st st, dec 1 st each end of 3rd, then every foll alt row until 3 sts rem.
Work 2 rows.
Work 3 tog, fasten off.

Finishing
Join body seam, fill. Join head seam, fill, then attach to body. Join hat seam, matching stripes and add a small pompom.

Sew tassels to ends of scarf. Join carrot nose seam, fill and attach open ended. Sew on coal eyes and coat buttons.

The snowman could be made larger by using thicker yarn and larger needles.

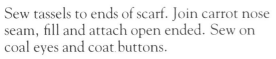

Christmas cameo

*Embroider this pretty little cameo to take pride of place in your
Christmas decorations. It would also make an acceptable present for
someone who appreciates fine handwork.*

Materials
Zweigart fabric 'Salamanca' in cream, 6in
(15cm) square
DMC stranded cotton – 1 skein each of red
57, yellow 94, pink 743, white and
random-dyed almond green
Crewel needle
Red Flexi-frame 3in (7.5cm) diameter
Thin card

Preparation
1 Trace the pattern and transfer to the
fabric.

2 Place the fabric in the Flexi-frame (if
desired).

Working the embroidery
3 Using two strands of thread together work
the embroidery following the key for colours
and stitches.

Making up
4 Remove the work from the frame and
lightly press on the back.

5 Using the frame as a guide, pencil a circle
on card. Cut out and place on wrong side of
the fabric, centring the design.

6 Lightly pencil round. Work basting
stitches round the circle ¼in (6mm) outside
the line. Draw up to fit embroidery over the
card circle. Trim all round. Finish thread
end with back stitches.

7 Put the mounted embroidery back in the
Flexi-frame.

8 Cut a circle of paper and glue to
the back of the embroidery if desired, but use
a white PVC adhesive sparingly.

KEY
1 Pink, red – Long and short stitch
2 Yellow – Long and short stitch
3 Almond green – Long and short stitch
4 Red – Long and short stitch
5 Pink – Long and short stitch
6 2 Almond, 1 white thread – French knots
7 White – French knots

Wise owls

There's nothing like a pair of owls to keep a little girl's ears warm on chilly days! These charming little toys could be made without the hair band as stocking filler gifts for young children.

Materials
8in (20cm) of 54in (137cm)-wide sand-coloured beaver fur fabric
8in (20cm) of 60in (152cm)-wide cream polished fur fabric
16in (40cm) of 36in (90cm)-wide green cotton fabric
8in (20cm) of medium-weight wadding
9in (23cm) square of beige felt
Four ⅝in (15mm) amber toy eyes
Plastic or metal hair band
Washable polyester toy filling

Preparation
1 Draw a pattern from the graph pattern on squared paper and put in all marks, words and numerals. Cut out the pattern pieces.

2 From the sand-coloured fur cut 4 owl shapes. From the cream-coloured fur cut 8 eye patches and 4 wings.

3 From the beige felt, cut 4 beaks and 8 claws.

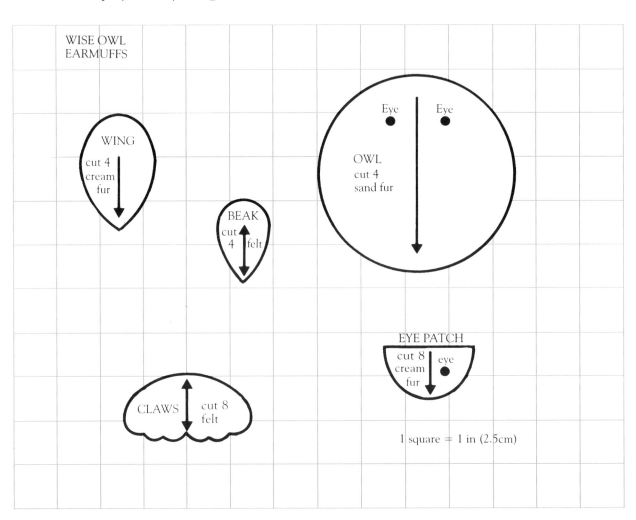

Making the earmuffs

4 Wrap a length of wadding around the hairband and hand sew the edges together. Cut a bias strip of green fabric to cover the hair band. Press under ¼in (6mm) on one long edge. Wrap around the hair band pinning the pressed edge over the long raw edge. Slipstitch the pressed edge in place.

5 Make tiny holes on 2 owls at the eye positions. Stitch each plain owl to one with eye holes leaving a gap at the top. Turn right side out.

6 Make tiny holes on 2 pairs of eye patches at the eye positions. Stitch each plain patch to one with eye holes along the straight edges. Insert the stalk of the eyes through the holes in the patches and fix through the holes on the owls.

7 Stuff the owls and insert the ends of the hair band inside. slipstitch the openings closed, sewing the owls securely to the hair band. Pin the wings to the sides of the owls and hand sew in position at the top edge.

8 Stitch the beaks and claws together in pairs leaving an opening to turn. Turn right side out and stuff. Slipstitch the openings closed. Hand sew the beaks to the owls' faces and the claws underneath the bases.

Lamb muff

Just the thing to keep the hands warm on a cold and frosty day – and such fun to carry around. The lamb's head purse is detachable.

Materials
½yd (45cm) of 54in (137cm)-wide cream curly fur
¼yd (20cm) of 54in (137cm)-wide black curly fur
½yd (45cm) of 36in (90cm)-wide cream lining
9in (23cm) square of black felt
½yd (45cm) of medium-weight wadding
12in (30cm) square of black lining
Two ⅜in (9mm) blue toy eyes
Three Velcro spot-ons
1¼yds (110cm) green cord
Washable polyester toy filling

Preparation
1 From the cream fur, cut out a rectangle 13½ × 12½in (34 × 31cm) for the muff and a piece of wadding 13½ × 10¼in (34 × 26cm). Tack the wadding to the wrong side of the muff 1⅛in (3cm) in from the ends.

2 From the black fur, cut out 4 rectangles for the legs 3½ × 3in (9 × 7.5cm) and from black felt, cut out 4 rectangles for the hooves 3 × 1⅝in (7.5 × 4cm). Stitch each leg to a hoof then fold lengthways in half and stitch the long edge and across the end of the hoof.

Making the muff
3 Turn legs right side out and stuff lightly. Baste across the upper edges. Baste 2 legs to the right side of the muff on one short edge 1⅝in (4cm) in from the ends and the remaining legs ¼in (6mm) in from first legs.

4 From the cream lining, cut out a rectangle 13½ × 8¼in (34 × 21cm). Stitch to the muff along the long edges and turn right side out. Fold the muff in half with the fur sides together and stitch the raw edges of the fur together, extending the stitching into the lining. Slipstitch remaining edges of lining together then turn fur to the outside.

5 Thread the cord through the muff. Place the ends side by side and bind tightly together with thread. Hand sew the join inside the muff.

Making the lamb's head purse
6 To make the purse, trace the head shape and cut out 1 face to the fold and 4 ears in black fur, 1 face in felt and 2 faces to the fold in black lining. Fix the eyes in place on the fur face then stitch each lining to a fur and felt face, leaving an opening to turn.

7 Turn right side out and slipstitch the openings closed. Pin the faces together with the linings facing. Fasten together with a Velcro spot-on between the dots on the upper edge then hand sew together around the outer edges between the dots.

8 Stitch the ears together in pairs, leaving an opening to turn. Turn right side out and sew to the purse at the dots. Attach the purse to the muff with two Velcro spot-ons.

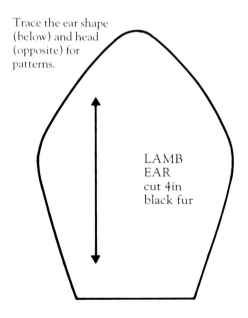

Trace the ear shape (below) and head (opposite) for patterns.

LAMB EAR
cut 4in
black fur

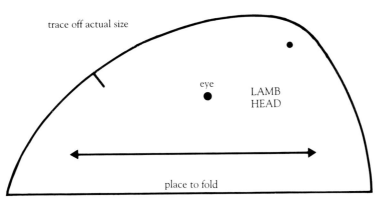

trace off actual size

eye

LAMB
HEAD

place to fold

Our thanks to the following for their designs:

Mary Lawrence *pp* 2–3, 24, 36, 52; Audrey Vincente Dean *pp* 12;
Pauline Butler *pp* 14, 74; Kerrie Dudley *pp* 50, 52, 54, 61;
Gail Lawther *pp* 18, 20, 56, 68; Cheryl Owen *pp* 92, 94;
Anna Griffiths *pp* 22, 66, 90; Lindy Tristram *pp* 26, 40, 42,
82; Lynette Mostaghimi *p* 84; Wendy Gardiner *pp* 16, 34,
58, 70; Hilary More *pp* 32, 38, 78, 80; Joy Gammon *pp* 10,
86, 88; Jasmin Suter *pp* 8, 28, 31, 44, 47.

Practical
Fish & Seafood

p^3

This is a P³ Book
This edition published in 2003

P³
Queen Street House
4 Queen Street
Bath BA1 1HE, UK

ISBN: 1-40540-548-1

Printed in China

NOTE

This book uses metric and imperial measurements. Follow the same units
of measurement throughout; do not mix metric and imperial.
All spoon measurements are level: teaspoons are assumed to be 5 ml, and
tablespoons are assumed to be 15 ml. Unless otherwise stated,
milk is assumed to be full fat, eggs and individual vegetables such as potatoes
are medium, and pepper is freshly ground black pepper.

The nutritional information provided for each recipe is per serving or per person.
Optional ingredients, variations or serving suggestions have
not been included in the calculations. The times given for each recipe are an approximate
guide only because the preparation times may differ according to the techniques used by
different people and the cooking times may vary as a result of the type of oven used.

Recipes using raw or very lightly cooked eggs should be
avoided by children, the elderly, pregnant women, convalescents,
and anyone suffering from an illness.

Contents

Introduction

Seafood deserves its image as a healthy food. It is rich in protein, and oily fish, such as mackerel and herring, are high in polyunsaturated fats (the type that help reduce cholesterol levels). White fish are a good source of minerals as well as low in fat, especially if poached, steamed or lightly grilled. Shellfish have been linked with high cholesterol, but they are also low in saturated fats and it is therefore healthy to eat them in moderation. The variety of fish and shellfish is staggering. You could eat seafood just once a week for a year without having the same dish twice. Seafood is quick and easy to prepare, making it an attractive ingredient for the busy cook. Many types of fish and most shellfish are sold ready to cook and so can be prepared in minutes. Fish is very good value for money in comparison with meat because there is much less waste: no fat to trim off or gristle to cut out. Making fish a regular part of your diet therefore makes a lot of sense.

Buying fish and shellfish

Wherever you shop for fish, at your trusted local fishmonger or at a supermarket, these guidelines apply:
- The eyes of the fish should be clear, bright and moist. Fish with dull, grey or cloudy eyes should be avoided.
- The gills should be bright red or pink, not dull or grey.
- Fish should smell of the sea and nothing else. Cooked shellfish should smell fresh, with no hint of ammonia. Check the use-by date if there is one.
- If you press the fish lightly with your thumb, the flesh should spring back, leaving little or no imprint.
- The shells of hinged shellfish, such as oysters, mussels and clams, should be tightly closed before cooking. If they are slightly open, tap them sharply. If they do not close, discard them.

Storage

You never know when fish was caught, especially if you buy it in a shop, so it is best to cook it on the day you buy it. If you are not planning to eat it straight away, put it in the refrigerator and do not keep it for more than a day or two. Refrigerators are not ideal places to store fish because they tend to have a temperature of about 5°C/38°F and fish is best kept at 0°C/32°F. Put the fish into a plastic container and scatter it with ice. Cover with clingfilm and store it in the coldest part of the refrigerator.

Firm-fleshed fish, such as turbot, Dover sole and monkfish, freeze better than less firm-fleshed fish such as sea bass, plaice and lemon sole, but all will deteriorate relatively quickly. Oily fish freezes least successfully, but if you need to keep it for more than a day or two, freezing is the best option. Thaw it thoroughly and slowly before cooking.

Preparation

The amount of preparation your fish needs depends on where you buy it. Supermarkets may have a wet fish counter with a trained fishmonger on hand, while other suppliers sell their fish vacuum-packed. Many fish are sold already scaled and gutted, and are often available either whole or filleted. A fishmonger will usually do the preparation for you, for a small charge. It is cheaper, however, to buy a whole fish and prepare it yourself. It is not difficult to do and just takes some practice.

Equipment

You need little special equipment for the recipes in this book, but if you are inspired by the dishes and plan to cook more fish, any of the following may prove a worthwhile purchase. If you want

to poach whole fish, a fish kettle would be a wise investment. This is an oblong, stainless-steel pan with a lifter and a lid, available in several sizes.

A wok – a Chinese pan with a heavy, rounded base – is useful for frying and stir-frying. For deep-frying you will need a deep-frying basket, a large frying pan and a thermometer. If you like to steam fish, think about buying a double boiler, a bamboo steamer or an electric steamer. If you intend to clean fish yourself, a good filleting knife is an essential tool. Tweezers are also useful for removing small bones.

Different cooking methods suit different fish but, as a general rule, poaching, steaming and stewing tend to produce a more moist result than grilling, baking or barbecuing. Drying out can be minimised, however, if the latter three methods are used at sufficiently high temperatures. This reduces moisture loss by ensuring the fish is cooked very quickly.

Poaching

The fish is immersed in a poaching liquid, which might be a court-bouillon, fish stock, milk, beer or cider. To poach successfully, bring the liquid to the boil and, as soon as it boils, remove the pan from the heat and let the fish finish cooking in the residual warmth. This method helps to prevent overcooking and is also excellent if you want to serve the fish cold.

Steaming

Both fish and shellfish benefit from being steamed. Again, a flavoured liquid can be used for the steaming, which will impart some of its flavour to the fish as it is being cooked. This method is especially good for keeping the fish moist and the flavour delicate. Steaming can be done in a fish kettle, a double boiler, or in a steamer inserted over a pan of boiling water.

Stewing

Whole fish or fish pieces can be cooked in liquid along with vegetables and other ingredients, as a stew. The fish flavours the liquid as it cooks.

Grilling and barbecuing

This is one of the quickest and easiest cooking methods for whole fish, steaks or fillets. Shellfish can also be grilled, but may need halving lengthways. For all these, the grill must be on its highest setting and the fish cooked as close to the heat source as possible.

A barbecue is also very useful for cooking fish. Brush the fish with butter, oil or a marinade before and during cooking to ensure that the flesh remains moist.

Baking and roasting

This covers all methods of cooking in the oven, including open roasting, casseroling and en papillote. This is a good method to choose for entertaining because, once the dish is in the oven, you are free to prepare other dishes.

Deep-frying

The fish may be coated in batter, flour or breadcrumbs and deep-fried in oil. You need a large, heavy-based saucepan or a deep-fryer. Large pieces of fish in batter are best cooked at a temperature of 180°C/350°F, which lets the fish cook without burning the batter. Fish pieces, such as goujons in breadcrumbs, should be cooked at 190°C/375°F. Drain deep-fried items well on kitchen paper so they remain crisp.

Shallow-frying or pan-frying

This is a quick method for cooking fish and shellfish, and can take as little as 3–4 minutes. A shallow layer of oil, or butter and oil, is heated in a frying pan, then the fish is added and cooked until just tender and lightly browned. A good frying pan is an essential piece of equipment.

KEY
Simplicity level 1–3 (1 easiest, 3 slightly harder)
Preparation time
Cooking time

Creamy Sweetcorn Soup

This speedy soup is a good storecupboard standby, made in a matter of minutes. If you prefer, you can use frozen crabsticks.

NUTRITIONAL INFORMATION

Calories 183   Sugars 9g
Protein ....7g   Fat 6g
Carbohydrate ...26g   Saturates 1g

5–10 mins   20 mins

SERVES 4

INGREDIENTS

1 tbsp vegetable oil

3 garlic cloves, crushed

1 tsp fresh root ginger, grated

700 ml/1¼ pints chicken stock

375 g/13 oz canned creamed sweetcorn

1 tbsp Thai fish sauce

175 g/6 oz canned white crab meat, drained

1 egg

salt and pepper

TO GARNISH

fresh coriander, shredded

paprika

1 Heat the oil in a large saucepan and add the crushed garlic. Cook for about 1 minute, stirring constantly.

2 Add the ginger to the pan, then stir in the stock and creamed sweetcorn. Bring the soup to the boil.

3 Stir in the fish sauce and crab meat. Season with salt and pepper, then return the soup to the boil.

4 Beat the egg, then stir lightly into the soup so that it sets into long strands. Simmer gently for about 30 seconds.

5 Ladle the soup into bowls. Serve hot, garnished with shredded coriander and with paprika sprinkled over.

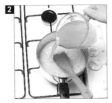

COOK'S TIP

To give the soup an extra-rich flavour for a special occasion, stir in 1 tablespoon of dry sherry or rice wine just before you ladle it into bowls.

Seafood Chowder

Mussels, an economical choice at the fishmonger, give essential flavour to this soup. The proportions of fish and prawns are flexible.

NUTRITIONAL INFORMATION

Calories	449	Sugars	.........4g
Protein	........34g	Fat	.........27g
Carbohydrate	...18g	Saturates	......16g

30 mins   40 mins

SERVES 6

I N G R E D I E N T S

1 kg/2 lb 4 oz mussels

4 tbsp plain flour

1.5 litres/2¾ pints fish stock

1 tbsp butter

1 large onion, finely chopped

350 g/12 oz skinless white fish fillets, such as cod, sole or haddock

200 g/7 oz cooked or raw peeled prawns

300 ml/10 fl oz whipping cream or double cream

salt and pepper

fresh dill, snipped, to garnish

1   Discard any broken mussels and those with open shells. Rinse, and pull off any 'beards'. Use a knife to scrape off any barnacles under cold running water. Put the mussels in a large, heavy-based saucepan with a little water. Cover tightly and cook over a high heat for 4 minutes or until the mussels open, shaking the pan occasionally. Remove the cooked mussels from their shells, adding any juices to the cooking liquid. Strain through a muslin-lined sieve and reserve.

2   Put the flour in a mixing bowl and very slowly whisk in enough stock to make a thick paste. Whisk in a little more stock to make a smooth liquid.

3   Melt the butter in a heavy-based saucepan over a medium-low heat. Add the onion, cover and cook for about 5 minutes, stirring, until it softens.

4   Add the remaining fish stock and bring to the boil. Slowly whisk in the flour mixture. Add the mussel cooking liquid. Season. Lower the heat and simmer, partially covered, for 15 minutes.

5   Add the fish and shellfish and simmer, stirring occasionally, for about 5 minutes or until the fish is cooked and begins to flake.

6   Stir in the prawns and cream. Taste and adjust the seasoning. Simmer for a few minutes more to heat through. Ladle into warm bowls, sprinkle the soup with fresh dill and serve.

Salmon & Leek Soup

Salmon is a favourite with almost everyone. This delicately flavoured and pretty soup is perfect for entertaining.

NUTRITIONAL INFORMATION

Calories	 338	Sugars	.... 7g
Protein	.... 19g	Fat	.... 22g
Carbohydrate	... 17g	Saturates	.... 8g

 10–15 mins   40 mins

SERVES 4

INGREDIENTS

1 tbsp olive oil

1 large onion, finely chopped

3 large leeks, including green parts, thinly sliced

1 potato, finely diced

450 ml/16 fl oz fish stock

700 ml/1¼ pints water

1 bay leaf

300 g/10½ oz skinless salmon fillet, cut into 1-cm/½-inch cubes

5 tbsp double cream

fresh lemon juice (optional)

salt and pepper

fresh chervil or parsley, snipped, to garnish

1 Heat the oil in a heavy-based saucepan over a medium heat. Add the onion and leeks and cook for about 3 minutes until they begin to soften.

2 Add the potato, stock, water and bay leaf with a large pinch of salt. Bring to the boil, lower the heat, cover and cook gently for about 25 minutes until the vegetables are tender. Remove and discard the bay leaf.

3 Let the soup cool slightly, then transfer about half of it to a blender or food processor and purée until smooth. (If using a food processor, strain off the cooking liquid and reserve. Purée half of the soup solids with enough cooking liquid to moisten them, then combine with the remaining liquid.)

4 Return the puréed soup to the saucepan and stir to blend. Reheat gently over a medium-low heat.

5 Season the salmon with salt and pepper and add to the soup. Continue cooking for about 5 minutes, stirring occasionally, until the fish is tender and starts to break up. Stir in the cream, then taste and adjust the seasoning, adding a little lemon juice if desired. Ladle into warm bowls, sprinkle with chervil or parsley and serve.

Saffron Fish Soup

This elegant soup makes a good dinner-party starter. To make planning easier, the saffron-flavoured soup base can be made ahead of time.

NUTRITIONAL INFORMATION

Calories 329   Sugars 8g
Protein . . . . .19g   Fat 18g
Carbohydrate . . .17g   Saturates 11g

10–15 mins   40 mins

SERVES 4

I N G R E D I E N T S

2 tsp butter

1 onion, finely chopped

1 leek, thinly sliced

1 carrot, thinly sliced

4 tbsp white rice

pinch of saffron threads

125 ml/4 fl oz dry white wine

1 litre/1¾ pints fish stock

125 ml/4 fl oz double cream

350 g/12 oz skinless white fish fillet, such as cod, haddock or monkfish, cut into 1-cm/½-inch cubes

4 tomatoes, skinned, deseeded and chopped

3 tbsp snipped fresh chives

salt and pepper

1 Put the butter in a saucepan and melt over a medium heat. Add the chopped onion, and sliced leek and carrot. Cook for 3–4 minutes, stirring frequently, until the onion is soft.

2 Add the rice, saffron, wine and stock, bring just to the boil, then reduce the heat to low. Season with salt and pepper to taste. Cover the pan and simmer for about 20 minutes, or until the rice and vegetables are soft.

3 Transfer the soup to a blender and purée until smooth, working in batches if necessary. (If using a food processor, strain off the cooking liquid and reserve. Purée the soup solids with enough cooking liquid to moisten them, then combine with the remaining liquid.)

4 Return the soup to the saucepan, stir in the cream and simmer over a low heat for a few minutes until heated through, stirring occasionally.

5 Season the fish and add, with the tomatoes, to the simmering soup. Cook for 3–5 minutes or until the fish is just tender.

6 Stir in most of the chives. Taste the soup and adjust the seasoning, if necessary. Ladle the soup into warm shallow bowls, sprinkle the remaining chives on top and serve.

Breton Fish Soup with Cider

Fishermen's soups are variable, depending on the season and the catch.
Monkfish has a texture like lobster, but tender cod is equally appealing.

NUTRITIONAL INFORMATION

Calories . . . . .103 Sugars 1.5g
Protein . . . . .5.2g Fat 6.3g
Carbohydrate . . .6.6g Saturates 3.8g

5–10 mins   40 mins

SERVES 4

INGREDIENTS

2 tsp butter

1 large leek, thinly sliced

2 shallots, finely chopped

300 ml/10 fl oz cider

125 ml/4 fl oz fish stock

250 g/9 oz potatoes, diced

1 bay leaf

4 tbsp plain flour

175 ml/6 fl oz milk

175 ml/6 fl oz double cream

55 g/2 oz fresh sorrel leaves

350 g/12 oz skinless monkfish or cod fillet,
cut into 2.5-cm/1-inch pieces

salt and pepper

COOK'S TIP

Be careful not to overcook the fish,
otherwise tender fish, such as cod,
breaks up into smaller and smaller
flakes, and firm fish, such as
monkfish, can become tough.

1 Melt the butter in a large saucepan over a medium-
low heat. Add the leek and shallots and then cook for
about 5 minutes, stirring frequently, until they start to
soften. Add the cider and bring to the boil.

2 Stir in the stock, potatoes and bay leaf with a large
pinch of salt (unless the stock is salty), and bring back
to the boil. Lower the heat, cover the pan and cook the
soup gently for 10 minutes.

3 Put the flour in a small bowl and very slowly whisk in
a few tablespoons of the milk to make a thick paste.
Stir in more milk, if needed, to make a smooth liquid.

4 Adjust the heat so that the soup bubbles gently. Stir
in the flour mixture and cook, stirring frequently,
for 5 minutes. Add the remaining milk and half the
cream. Continue cooking for about 10 minutes until the
potatoes are tender.

5 Finely chop the sorrel and combine with the remaining
cream. (If using a food processor, add the sorrel and
chop, then add the cream and process briefly.)

6 Stir the sorrel cream into the soup and add the fish.
Continue cooking, stirring occasionally, for about
3 minutes until the monkfish stiffens or the cod just begins
to flake. Taste the soup and adjust the seasoning, if
necessary. Ladle into warm bowls and serve.

Skate & Spinach Salad

This colourful fish salad makes a satisfying main course. Skate should smell fresh, so if a fish has a strong odour of ammonia do not use it.

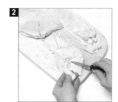

NUTRITIONAL INFORMATION

Calories 316	Sugars 18g	
Protein 32g	Fat 13g	
Carbohydrate . . .18g	Saturates 1g	

15 mins   40 mins

SERVES 4

I N G R E D I E N T S

700 g/1 lb 9 oz skate wings, trimmed

2 sprigs fresh rosemary

1 fresh or dried bay leaf

1 tbsp black peppercorns

1 lemon, cut into quarters

450 g/1 lb baby spinach leaves

1 tbsp olive oil

1 small red onion, thinly sliced

2 garlic cloves, crushed

½ tsp chilli flakes

50 g/1¾ oz pine kernels, lightly toasted

50 g/1¾ oz raisins

1 tbsp brown sugar

2 tbsp chopped fresh parsley

1 Put the skate wings into a large saucepan with the rosemary, bay leaf, peppercorns and lemon pieces. Cover with cold water and bring to the boil. Simmer, covered, for 4–5 minutes until the flesh begins to come away from the cartilage. Remove from the heat and leave to stand for 15 minutes.

2 Lift the fish from the poaching water and remove the flesh by shredding it off. Set aside.

3 In a clean saucepan, cook the spinach (with just the water that clings to the leaves after washing) over a high heat for 30 seconds until just wilted. Drain, refresh under cold water and drain well again. Squeeze out excess water and set aside.

4 Heat the olive oil in a large, deep frying pan. Add the red onion and cook for 3–4 minutes until softened but not browned. Add the garlic, chilli flakes, pine kernels, raisins and sugar. Cook for 1–2 minutes, then add the spinach and toss for 1 minute until heated through.

5 Gently fold in the skate and cook for another minute. Season well.

6 Divide the salad between 4 serving plates and sprinkle with the chopped parsley. Serve immediately.

Smoked Mackerel Pâté

This is a quick and easy pâté with plenty of flavour. It originates from Goa, on the west coast of India, an area famous for its seafood.

NUTRITIONAL INFORMATION

Calories	316	Sugars	.........3g
Protein	........13g	Fat	..........23g
Carbohydrate	...14g	Saturates	.......8g

25–30 mins, plus refrigeration time   5–10 mins

SERVES 4

I N G R E D I E N T S

200 g/7 oz smoked mackerel fillet

1 small, hot green chilli, deseeded and chopped

1 garlic clove, chopped

3 tbsp fresh coriander leaves

150 ml/5 fl oz soured cream

1 small red onion, chopped

2 tbsp lime juice

4 slices white bread, crusts removed

salt and pepper

1 Skin and flake the mackerel fillet, removing any small bones. Put the flesh in the bowl of a food processor along with the chilli, garlic, coriander and soured cream. Blend until smooth.

2 Transfer the mixture to a bowl and mix in the onion and lime juice. Season to taste. The pâté will seem very soft at this stage but will firm up in the refrigerator. Refrigerate for several hours, or overnight if possible.

3 The pâté is served with melba toast. To make it, place the trimmed bread slices under a preheated medium grill and toast lightly on both sides. Split each piece in half horizontally, then cut across diagonally to form 4 triangles per slice.

4 Put the melba toast triangles, untoasted side up, under the grill and toast them until they are golden and curled at the edges. Serve the toast warm or cold with the pâté.

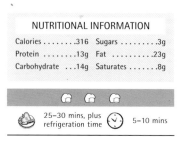

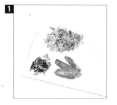

Thai Fishcakes

These little fishcakes are very popular in Thailand as street food, and make a perfect snack. Alternatively, serve them as a starter.

NUTRITIONAL INFORMATION

Calories . . . . . . .205 Sugars 6g
Protein . . . . .17g Fat 12g
Carbohydrate . . . .7g Saturates 2g

5–10 mins   30–40 mins

SERVES 4-5

I N G R E D I E N T S

350 g/12 oz white fish fillet without skin,
   such as cod or haddock

1 tbsp Thai fish sauce

2 tsp Thai red curry paste

1 tbsp lime juice

1 garlic clove, crushed

4 dried kaffir lime leaves, crumbled

1 egg white

3 tbsp chopped fresh coriander

vegetable oil, for cooking

salt and pepper

fresh salad leaves, to serve

P E A N U T   D I P

1 small red chilli

1 tbsp light soy sauce

1 tbsp lime juice

1 tbsp brown sugar

3 tbsp chunky peanut butter

4 tbsp coconut milk

1 Put the fish fillet in a food processor with the fish sauce, red curry paste, lime juice, garlic, lime leaves and egg white and process the ingredients until a smooth paste forms.

2 Stir in the fresh coriander and quickly process the paste again until it is mixed. Divide the fish mixture into about 8–10 pieces and roll into balls, then flatten the balls to make round patties and set them aside.

3 To make the peanut dip, halve and deseed the chilli, then chop finely. Place in a small pan with the remaining dip ingredients and heat gently, stirring constantly, until blended. Season to taste.

4 Heat the oil in a frying pan and cook the fishcakes for 3–4 minutes on each side until golden brown (you may need to do this in batches). Drain on kitchen paper and serve hot on a bed of salad leaves with the peanut dip.

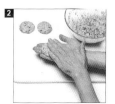

Gravadlax

You need two pieces of salmon fillet approximately the same size for this dish. Ask your fishmonger to remove all the bones and scale the fish.

NUTRITIONAL INFORMATION

Calories 608   Sugars 11g
Protein . . . . .37g   Fat 34g
Carbohydrate . . .41g   Saturates 14g

 30–40 mins, plus 2 days chilling   0 mins

SERVES 6

I N G R E D I E N T S

2 salmon fillets, about 450 g/1 lb each, skin left on

6 tbsp roughly chopped fresh dill

115 g/4 oz sea salt

50 g/1¾ oz sugar

1 tbsp roughly crushed white peppercorns

12 slices brown bread, buttered, to serve

G A R N I S H

lemon slices

sprigs of fresh dill

1 Rinse the salmon fillets and dry with kitchen paper. Put one fillet, skin-side down, in a non-metallic dish.

2 Mix together the dill, sea salt, sugar and peppercorns. Spread this mixture over the first fillet of fish and place the second fillet, skin-side up, on top. Put a plate, the same size as the fish, on top and put a weight on the plate (3 or 4 cans of tomatoes or similar will do).

3 Refrigerate for 2 days, turning the salmon fillets about every 12 hours and basting with any juices that have come out of the fish.

4 Remove the salmon from the brine and slice thinly, without slicing the skin, as you would smoked salmon. Cut the brown bread into triangles and serve with the salmon. Garnish with lemon wedges and sprigs of fresh dill.

COOK'S TIP

You can brush the marinade off the salmon before slicing, but the line of green along the edge of the salmon is quite attractive and, of course, full of flavour.

Thai-style Crab Sandwich

A hearty, open sandwich, topped with a classic flavour combination –
crab with avocado and ginger. Perfect for a light summer lunch.

NUTRITIONAL INFORMATION

Calories	768	Sugars	.........3g
Protein	........26g	Fat	..........49g
Carbohydrate	...58g	Saturates	.......8g

40 mins   0 mins

SERVES 2

I N G R E D I E N T S

2 tbsp lime juice

2-cm/¾-inch piece fresh root ginger, grated

2-cm/¾-inch piece lemon grass,
  finely chopped

5 tbsp mayonnaise

2 large slices crusty bread

1 ripe avocado

150 g/5½ oz cooked crab meat

freshly ground black pepper

sprigs of fresh coriander, to garnish

 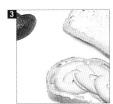 

COOK'S TIP

To make mayonnaise flavoured
with lime and ginger, place 2 egg
yolks, 1 tablespoon lime juice and
½ teaspoon grated root ginger in a
blender. With the motor running,
gradually add 300 ml/10 fl oz
olive oil, drop by drop, until the
mixture is thick and smooth.
Season with salt and pepper.

1 Mix half the lime juice with the ginger
and lemon grass. Add 1 tablespoon of
mayonnaise and mix well.

2 Spread 1 tablespoon of mayonnaise
smoothly over each slice of bread.

3 Halve the avocado and remove the
stone. Peel and slice the flesh thinly,
then arrange the slices on the bread.
Sprinkle with lime juice.

4 Spoon the crab meat over the
avocado, then add the remaining
lime juice. Spoon over the remaining
mayonnaise, season with freshly ground
black pepper, top with coriander sprigs and
serve immediately.

Swordfish or Tuna Fajitas

Fajitas are usually made with chicken or lamb but using a firm fish like swordfish or tuna works very well.

NUTRITIONAL INFORMATION

Calories	766	Sugars	........12g
Protein	........52g	Fat	..........36g
Carbohydrate	...63g	Saturates	......10g

30 mins, plus 1–2 hrs marinating   20 mins

SERVES 4

I N G R E D I E N T S

3 tbsp olive oil

2 tsp chilli powder

1 tsp ground cumin

pinch cayenne pepper

1 garlic clove, crushed

900 g/2 lb swordfish or tuna steaks

1 red pepper, deseeded and thinly sliced

1 yellow pepper, deseeded and thinly sliced

2 courgettes, cut into batons

1 large onion, thinly sliced

12 soft flour tortillas

1 tbsp lemon juice

3 tbsp chopped fresh coriander

salt and pepper

150 ml/5 fl oz soured cream, to serve

G U A C A M O L E

1 large avocado

1 tomato, skinned, deseeded and diced

1 garlic clove, crushed

dash of Tabasco

2 tbsp lemon juice

salt and pepper

1 In a bowl, mix together the oil, chilli powder, cumin, cayenne and garlic. Cut the fish into chunks and mix with the marinade. Set aside for 1–2 hours.

2 Heat a large frying pan until hot. Put in the fish and its marinade and cook for 2 minutes, stirring occasionally, until the fish begins to brown. Add the peppers, courgettes and onion and cook for another 5 minutes until the vegetables have softened but all are still firm.

3 Meanwhile, gently warm the tortillas in an oven or microwave.

4 To make the guacamole, mash the avocado in a bowl. Stir in the tomato, garlic, Tabasco, lemon juice and seasoning.

5 Add the lemon juice, coriander and seasoning to the vegetable mix. Spoon some of the mixture onto the warmed tortillas. Top each one with guacamole and a spoonful of soured cream and roll up.

Steamed Yellow Fish Fillets

Thailand has an abundance of fresh fish, which is an important part of the local diet. Dishes such as these steamed fillets are popular.

NUTRITIONAL INFORMATION

Calories 165   Sugars 1g
Protein ....23g   Fat 2g
Carbohydrate ...13g   Saturates 1g

40 mins   15 mins

SERVES 3-4

INGREDIENTS

500 g/1 lb 2 oz firm fish fillets, such as red snapper, sole or monkfish

1 dried red bird's-eye chilli

1 small onion, chopped

3 garlic cloves, chopped

2 sprigs fresh coriander

1 tsp coriander seeds

½ tsp turmeric

½ tsp freshly ground black pepper

1 tbsp Thai fish sauce

2 tbsp coconut milk

1 small egg, beaten

2 tbsp rice flour

strips of red and green chilli, to garnish

soy sauce, to serve

1 Remove any skin from the fish and cut the fillets diagonally into long 2-cm/¾-inch wide strips.

2 Place the dried chilli in a mortar. Add the onion, garlic, fresh coriander and coriander seeds and grind with a pestle until they make a smooth paste.

3 Add the turmeric, black pepper, fish sauce, coconut milk and beaten egg and stir well to mix evenly.

4 Dip the fish strips into the paste mixture, then into the rice flour to coat lightly.

5 Bring the water in a steamer to the boil, then arrange the fish strips in the top of the steamer. Cover and steam for about 12–15 minutes until the fish is just firm.

6 Serve the fish with soy sauce and an accompaniment of stir-fried vegetables or salad.

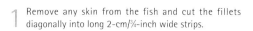
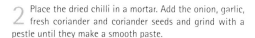

COOK'S TIP

If you don't have a steamer, improvise by placing a large metal colander over a large pan of boiling water and cover with an upturned plate to enclose the fish as it steams.

Cotriade

This is a rich French stew of fish and vegetables, flavoured with saffron and herbs. The fish and vegetables, and the soup, are served separately.

NUTRITIONAL INFORMATION

Calories	81	Sugars	.......0.9g
Protein	........7.4g	Fat	..........3.9g
Carbohydrate	...3.8g	Saturates	.....1.1g

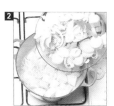

15 mins   40 mins

SERVES 6

I N G R E D I E N T S

large pinch saffron

600 ml/1 pint hot fish stock

1 tbsp olive oil

2 tbsp butter

1 onion, sliced

2 garlic cloves, chopped

1 leek, sliced

1 small fennel bulb, finely sliced

450 g/1 lb potatoes, cut into chunks

150 ml/5 fl oz dry white wine

1 tbsp fresh thyme leaves

2 bay leaves

4 ripe tomatoes, skinned and chopped

900 g/2 lb mixed fish such as haddock, hake, mackerel or red snapper, roughly chopped

2 tbsp chopped fresh parsley

salt and pepper

lemon slices and crusty bread, to serve

1 Using a mortar and pestle, crush the saffron and add it to the fish stock. Stir the mixture and leave to infuse for at least 10 minutes.

2 In a large saucepan, heat the oil and butter together. Add the onion and cook gently for 4–5 minutes until softened. Add the garlic, leek, fennel and potatoes. Cover and cook for another 10–15 minutes until the vegetables have softened.

3 Add the wine and simmer rapidly for 3–4 minutes until it has reduced by half. Add the thyme, bay leaves and tomatoes and stir well. Add the saffron-infused stock. Bring to the boil, cover and simmer gently for 15 minutes until the vegetables are tender.

4 Add the fish, return to the boil and simmer for another 3–4 minutes until the fish is tender. Add the parsley and season to taste. Using a slotted spoon, remove the fish and vegetables to a warmed serving dish. Serve the soup with lemon slices and plenty of crusty bread.

Basque Tuna Stew

Although versions of this stew are eaten throughout Spain, it originated in the northern Basque region.

NUTRITIONAL INFORMATION

Calories 110   Sugars 8g
Protein ....10g   Fat 2g
Carbohydrate ...13g   Saturates 0g

10–15 mins   40 mins

SERVES 4

INGREDIENTS

5 tbsp olive oil

1 large onion, chopped

2 garlic cloves, chopped

200 g/7 oz canned chopped tomatoes

700 g/1 lb 9 oz potatoes, cut into
    5-cm/2-inch chunks

3 green peppers, deseeded and
    roughly chopped

300 ml/10 fl oz cold water

900 g/2 lb fresh tuna, cut into chunks

4 slices crusty white bread

salt and pepper

VARIATION

Substitute any very firm-fleshed fish, such as shark or swordfish, for the tuna used in this recipe.

 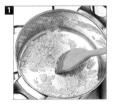 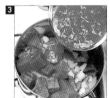 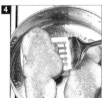

1 Heat 2 tablespoons of the olive oil in a saucepan and add the onion. Cook for 8–10 minutes until soft and brown. Add the garlic and cook for another minute, then add the tomatoes. Cover and simmer for 30 minutes until thickened.

2 Meanwhile, in a clean saucepan, mix together the potatoes and peppers. Add the water (which should just cover the vegetables). Bring to the boil and simmer for 15 minutes until the potatoes are almost cooked through.

3 Add the tuna and the tomato mixture to the potatoes and peppers and season. Cover the pan and simmer for 6–8 minutes until the tuna is tender.

4 Meanwhile, heat the remaining oil in a large frying pan over a medium heat and add the bread slices. Cook them on both sides until golden. Drain on kitchen paper. Serve with the stew.

Sardines with Pesto

This is a very quick and tasty midweek supper dish. Use a good-quality ready-made pesto for an even speedier meal.

NUTRITIONAL INFORMATION

Calories	617	Sugars	.......0.1g
Protein	........27g	Fat	..........56g
Carbohydrate	....1g	Saturates	......11g

 30 mins   10 mins

SERVES 4

I N G R E D I E N T S

16 large sardines, scaled and gutted

50 g/1¾ oz fresh basil leaves

2 garlic cloves, crushed

2 tbsp pine kernels, toasted

50 g/1¾ oz Parmesan cheese, freshly grated

150 ml/5 fl oz olive oil

salt and pepper

lemon slices, to serve

1 Wash and dry the sardines and arrange on a grill pan.

2 Put the basil leaves, garlic and pine kernels in a food processor. Blend until finely chopped. Scrape the mixture out of the food processor, put it in a bowl and stir in the Parmesan cheese and olive oil. Season to taste.

3 Spread a little of the pesto sauce over one side of the sardines and place under a preheated hot grill for 3 minutes. Turn the fish, spread with more pesto and grill for another 3 minutes until the sardines are cooked.

4 Serve immediately with extra pesto and lemon slices.

VARIATION

This treatment will also work well with other small oily fish such as herrings and pilchards.

Seared Tuna Steaks

Meaty tuna steaks have enough flavour to stand up to the robust taste of anchovies. Serve these with pan-fried potatoes or a mixed rice dish.

NUTRITIONAL INFORMATION

Calories ....564 Sugars 0g
Protein ....55g Fat 38g
Carbohydrate ....0g Saturates 19g

 35 mins   5 mins

SERVES 4

I N G R E D I E N T S

olive oil

4 thick tuna steaks, each about
    225 g/8 oz and 2 cm/¾ inch thick

salt and pepper

A N C H O V Y   B U T T E R

8 anchovy fillets in oil, drained

4 spring onions, finely chopped

1 tbsp finely grated orange zest

115 g/4 oz unsalted butter, softened

¼ tsp lemon juice

pepper

T O   G A R N I S H

sprigs of fresh flat-leaved parsley

strips of orange zest

1 To make the anchovy butter, chop the anchovies very finely and put them in a bowl with the spring onions, orange zest and softened butter. Beat well until all the ingredients are blended. Season with lemon juice and pepper to taste.

2 Place the flavoured butter on a sheet of baking paper and then roll it up into a log shape. Fold over the ends of the paper carefully to seal in the butter, then place the package in the freezer for about 15 minutes to firm.

3 Heat a ridged grill pan over a high heat. Lightly brush with olive oil, add the tuna steaks and cook for 2 minutes, in batches if necessary. Turn the steaks over and cook for 2 more minutes for rare, or up to 4 minutes for well done. Season to taste with salt and pepper.

4 Transfer the fish to a warm plate and put 2 thin slices of anchovy butter on each of the tuna steaks. Garnish with fresh parsley sprigs and orange zest, and serve the dish at once.

VARIATION

If you particularly like hot, spicy food, add a pinch of dried chilli flakes to the butter mixture.

Prawn Rostis

These crisp little vegetable and prawn cakes make an ideal light lunch or supper, accompanied by a salad.

NUTRITIONAL INFORMATION

Calories 445   Sugars 9g
Protein ....19g   Fat 29g
Carbohydrate ...29g   Saturates 4g

🥔 10 mins   🕐 1 hr

SERVES 4

I N G R E D I E N T S

350 g/12 oz potatoes

350 g/12 oz celeriac

1 carrot

½ small onion

225 g/8 oz prawns, cooked and peeled, thawed if frozen and well drained on kitchen paper

2½ tbsp plain flour

1 egg, lightly beaten

vegetable oil, for cooking

salt and pepper

C H E R R Y   T O M A T O   S A L S A

225 g/8 oz mixed cherry tomatoes such as baby plum, yellow, orange or pear, cut into quarters

½ small mango, finely diced

1 red chilli, deseeded and finely chopped

½ small red onion, finely chopped

1 tbsp chopped fresh coriander

1 tbsp chopped fresh chives

2 tbsp olive oil

2 tsp lemon juice

salt and pepper

1 For the salsa, mix the tomatoes in a bowl with the mango, chilli, onion, coriander, chives, olive oil, lemon juice and seasoning. Set aside to infuse.

2 Using a food processor or the fine blade of a box grater, finely grate the potatoes, celeriac, carrot and onion. Mix together in a bowl with the prawns, flour and egg. Season well and set aside.

3 Divide the prawn mixture into eight equal pieces. Press each piece into a greased 10-cm/4-inch biscuit cutter (if you have only one cutter, you can simply shape the rostis individually).

4 In a large frying pan, heat a shallow layer of oil. When hot, transfer the vegetable cakes, still in the cutters if possible, to the frying pan, in batches if necessary. When the oil sizzles underneath, remove the cutter. Cook gently, pressing down with a palette knife, for 6–8 minutes on each side until crisp and browned and the vegetables are tender. Drain on kitchen paper and keep warm in a preheated oven. Serve the rostis hot with the tomato salsa.

Seafood Lasagne

A rich dish of layers of pasta, with seafood and mushrooms in a tomato sauce, topped with béchamel sauce and baked until golden.

NUTRITIONAL INFORMATION

Calories 790   Sugars 23g
Protein . . . . .55g   Fat 32g
Carbohydrate . . .74g   Saturates 19g

30 mins   1 hr 20 mins

SERVES 6

I N G R E D I E N T S

4 tbsp butter, plus extra for greasing

6 tbsp flour

1 tsp mustard powder

600 ml/1 pint milk

2 tbsp olive oil

1 onion, chopped

2 garlic cloves, finely chopped

1 tbsp fresh thyme leaves

450 g/1 lb mixed mushrooms, sliced

150 ml/5 fl oz white wine

400 g/14 oz canned chopped tomatoes

450 g/1 lb skinless mixed white fish fillets, cubed

225 g/8 oz fresh scallops, trimmed

4–6 sheets fresh lasagne

225 g/8 oz mozzarella cheese, drained and chopped

salt and pepper

 1 Melt the butter in a saucepan. Add the flour and mustard powder and stir until smooth. Simmer gently for 2 minutes without colouring. Gradually stir in the milk, whisking until smooth. Bring to the boil and simmer for 2 minutes. Remove from the heat, transfer to a bowl and cover the surface of the sauce with clingfilm to prevent a skin from forming. Set aside.

2 Heat the oil in a frying pan and add the onion, garlic and thyme. Cook gently for 5 minutes until softened. Add the mushrooms and cook for an additional 5 minutes until softened. Stir in the wine and boil rapidly until nearly evaporated. Stir in the tomatoes. Bring to the boil and simmer, covered, for 15 minutes. Season and set aside.

3 Grease a lasagne dish. Spoon half of the tomato sauce in the dish and top with half the fish and scallops.

4 Layer half of the lasagne over the fish, pour over half of the white sauce and then add half of the mozzarella. Repeat these layers, finishing with the white sauce and mozzarella.

5 Bake the lasagne in a preheated oven at 200°C/400°F/Gas Mark 6 for about 35–40 minutes until the top is bubbling and golden and the fish is cooked through. Remove the dish from the oven and leave to stand on a heat-resistant surface or mat for about 10 minutes before serving.

Thai Noodles

This classic Thai noodle dish is flavoured with fish sauce, roasted peanuts and tiger prawns.

NUTRITIONAL INFORMATION

Calories ....344 Sugars 2g
Protein ....21g Fat 17g
Carbohydrate ...27g Saturates 2g

🍲 15 mins   🕐 30 mins

SERVES 4

I N G R E D I E N T S

350 g/12 oz tiger prawns, peeled

115 g/4 oz flat rice noodles or
    rice vermicelli

4 tbsp vegetable oil

2 garlic cloves, finely chopped

1 egg

2 tbsp lemon juice

1½ tbsp Thai fish sauce

½ tsp sugar

2 tbsp chopped roasted peanuts

50 g/1¾ oz fresh beansprouts

½ tsp cayenne pepper

2 spring onions, cut into 2.5-cm/1-inch
    pieces

1 tbsp chopped fresh coriander

lemon wedges, to serve

VARIATION

This is a basic dish to which lots of different cooked seafood could be added. Cooked squid rings, mussels and langoustines would all work just as well.

1 Drain the prawns on kitchen paper to remove excess moisture. Set aside. Cook the rice noodles or rice vermicelli according to the packet instructions. Drain well and set aside.

2 Heat the oil in a wok or large frying pan and then add the chopped garlic. Cook until the garlic is just golden. Add the egg and stir quickly to break it up. Cook for a few seconds.

3 Add the prawns and noodles, scraping down the sides of the pan to ensure they mix with the egg and garlic.

4 Add the lemon juice, fish sauce, sugar, half the peanuts and beansprouts, and all the cayenne pepper and spring onions, stirring quickly all the time. Cook over a high heat for another 4 minutes until everything is heated through.

5 Turn onto serving plates. Top with the remaining peanuts and beansprouts and sprinkle with the coriander. Serve with lemon wedges.

Kedgeree

Originally, kedgeree or *khichri* was a Hindu dish of rice and lentils, varied with fish or meat in all kinds of ways.

NUTRITIONAL INFORMATION

Calories	457	Sugars	.........3g
Protein	........33g	Fat	..........18g
Carbohydrate	...40g	Saturates	.......6g

10–15 mins   30 mins

SERVES 4

INGREDIENTS

450 g/1 lb undyed smoked haddock fillet

2 tbsp olive oil

1 large onion, chopped

2 garlic cloves, finely chopped

½ tsp ground turmeric

½ tsp ground cumin

1 tsp ground coriander

175 g/6 oz basmati rice

4 medium eggs

2 tbsp butter

1 tbsp chopped fresh parsley

TO SERVE

lemon wedges

mango chutney

1 Pour boiling water over the haddock fillet and leave to stand for 10 minutes. Lift the fish from the cooking water, discard the skin and bones and flake the fish. Set aside. Reserve the cooking water.

2 Heat the oil in a large pan and add the onion. Cook for 10 minutes over a medium heat until starting to brown. Add the garlic and cook for an additional 30 seconds. Add the turmeric, cumin and coriander and stir-fry for 30 seconds until the spices smell fragrant. Add the rice and stir well.

3 Measure out 350 ml/12 fl oz of the haddock cooking water and add this to the saucepan. Stir well and bring to the boil. Cover the pan and cook over a very low heat for 12–15 minutes until the rice is tender and the liquid is absorbed.

4 Meanwhile, bring a small saucepan of water to the boil and place the eggs carefully in the water. When the water has returned to the boil, cook the eggs for 8 minutes. Drain them immediately and refresh under cold water to stop them from cooking. Set them to one side.

5 Add the reserved pieces of haddock, the butter and the fresh parsley to the rice. Turn the rice onto a large serving dish. Shell the hard-boiled eggs, cut them into quarters and arrange them on top of the rice. Serve the kedgeree with lemon wedges and mango chutney.

 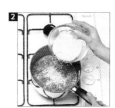 

Moules Marinières

The Spanish, French and Italians all serve variations of this simple mussel recipe, which is universally popular. Use the freshest mussels you can find.

NUTRITIONAL INFORMATION

Calories 278	Sugars 6g	
Protein 18g	Fat 14g	
Carbohydrate ...10g	Saturates 2g	

30 mins • 25 mins

SERVES 4

INGREDIENTS

2 kg/4 lb 8 oz live mussels

4 tbsp olive oil

4–6 large garlic cloves, halved

800 g/1 lb 12 oz canned chopped tomatoes

300 ml/10 fl oz dry white wine

2 tbsp finely chopped fresh flat-leaved parsley, plus extra to garnish

1 tbsp finely chopped fresh oregano

salt and pepper

French bread, to serve

1 Leave the mussels to soak in a bowl of lightly salted water for 30 minutes. Rinse them under cold, running water and lightly scrub to remove any sand from the shells. Using a small, sharp knife, remove the 'beards' from the shells.

2 Discard any broken mussels or open mussels that do not shut when tapped firmly with the back of a knife. This indicates they are dead and could cause food poisoning if eaten. Rinse the mussels again, then set aside in a colander.

3 Heat the olive oil in a large saucepan or pot over a medium-high heat. Add the garlic and cook, stirring, for about 3 minutes to flavour the oil. Using a slotted spoon, remove the garlic from the pan.

4 Add the tomatoes and their juice, the wine, parsley and oregano, and bring to the boil, stirring. Lower the heat, cover and simmer for 5 minutes to allow the flavours to blend.

5 Add the mussels, cover and simmer for 5–8 minutes, shaking the pan regularly until they open. Using a slotted spoon, transfer them to serving bowls, discarding any that are not open.

6 Season the sauce with salt and pepper to taste. Ladle the sauce over the mussels, sprinkle with extra parsley and serve at once with plenty of French bread to soak up the delicious juices.

Tuna in Sweet-&-Sour Sauce

Tuna is a firm, meaty-textured fish. You can also use shark or mackerel with this rich and delicious sauce.

NUTRITIONAL INFORMATION

Calories	...303	Sugars	...12g
Protein	...31g	Fat	...12g
Carbohydrate	...20g	Saturates	...3g

30 mins — 20 mins

SERVES 4

INGREDIENTS

4 fresh tuna steaks, about 500 g/1 lb 2 oz total weight

¼ tsp freshly ground black pepper

2 tbsp groundnut oil

1 onion, diced

1 small red pepper, deseeded and cut into short, thin sticks

1 garlic clove, crushed

1 tbsp brown sugar

½ cucumber, deseeded and cut into short, thin sticks

2 pineapple slices, diced

1 tsp finely chopped fresh root ginger

1 tbsp cornflour

1½ tbsp lime juice

1 tbsp Thai fish sauce

250 ml/9 fl oz fish stock

lime and cucumber slices, to garnish

1 Sprinkle the tuna steaks with black pepper on both sides and brush with a little of the oil. Heat a heavy frying pan or ridged grill pan. Arrange the tuna steaks on the pan and cook for about 8 minutes, turning them over once during cooking.

2 Heat the remaining oil in another pan and fry the onion, red pepper and garlic gently for 3–4 minutes to soften.

3 Remove from the heat, then stir in the sugar, cucumber, pineapple slices and chopped ginger.

4 In a separate bowl, blend the cornflour with the lime juice and fish sauce, then stir in the stock and add to the pan. Stir over a medium heat until boiling, then cook for 1–2 minutes until thickened and clear.

5 Spoon the sauce over the tuna and serve garnished with slices of lime and cucumber.

Poached Rainbow Trout

This colourful dish is served cold and makes a lovely summer lunch or supper dish. If watercress is unavailable, use baby spinach instead.

NUTRITIONAL INFORMATION

Calories 99	Sugars 1.1g	
Protein 5.7g	Fat 6.3g	
Carbohydrate ...3.7g	Saturates 1g	

 10 mins   1 hr 5 mins

SERVES 4

I N G R E D I E N T S

1.3 kg/3 lb rainbow trout fillets, cleaned

700 g/1 lb 9 oz new potatoes, halved

3 spring onions, finely chopped

1 egg, hard-boiled and chopped

C O U R T - B O U I L L O N

850 ml/1½ pints cold water

850 ml/1½ pints dry white wine

3 tbsp white wine vinegar

2 large carrots, roughly chopped

1 onion, roughly chopped

2 celery sticks, roughly chopped

2 leeks, roughly chopped

2 garlic cloves, roughly chopped

2 fresh or dried bay leaves

4 sprigs fresh parsley

4 sprigs fresh thyme

6 black peppercorns

1 tsp salt

M A Y O N N A I S E

1 egg yolk

1 tsp Dijon mustard

1 tsp white wine vinegar

55 g/2 oz watercress leaves, chopped

225 ml/8 fl oz light olive oil

salt and pepper

1 Place the court-bouillon ingredients in a large pan, cover and simmer for 30 minutes. Strain through a fine sieve into a clean pan. Bring to the boil again and simmer fast, uncovered, for 15–20 minutes until reduced to 600 ml/1 pint.

2 Place the trout in a frying pan. Add the court-bouillon and bring slowly to the boil. Remove from the heat and leave in the poaching liquid to go cold.

3 To make the mayonnaise, put the egg yolk, mustard, vinegar, watercress and seasoning into a food processor and blend for 30 seconds until foaming. Add the olive oil, drop by drop, until the mixture begins to thicken. Continue adding the oil in a slow stream until incorporated. Add a little hot water if it is too thick. Season and set aside.

4 Cook the potatoes in boiling water for 12–15 minutes. Drain and refresh under cold running water. Set aside.

5 Toss the cold potatoes with the watercress mayonnaise, spring onions and hard-boiled egg.

6 Lift the fish from the poaching liquid and drain on kitchen paper. Carefully pull the skin away from the trout. Serve immediately with the potato salad.

Hake Steaks with Chermoula

The cooking time may seem long and indeed you could decrease it slightly if you prefer, but in Morocco they like their fish well cooked.

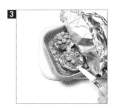

NUTRITIONAL INFORMATION

Calories	590	Sugars	.........1g
Protein	........42g	Fat	..........46g
Carbohydrate	....2g	Saturates	.......7g

10 mins, plus marinating

35–40 mins

SERVES 4

INGREDIENTS

4 hake steaks, about 225 g/8 oz each

115 g/4 oz stoned green olives

selection of freshly cooked vegetables, to serve

MARINADE

6 tbsp finely chopped fresh coriander

6 tbsp finely chopped fresh parsley

6 garlic cloves, crushed

1 tbsp ground cumin

1 tsp ground coriander

1 tbsp paprika

pinch cayenne pepper

150 ml/5 fl oz fresh lemon juice

300 ml/10 fl oz olive oil

1 For the marinade, put all the ingredients in a small bowl and then mix together well.

2 Wash and dry the hake steaks and place them in an ovenproof dish. Pour the marinade over the fish and leave for at least 1 hour and preferably overnight.

3 Before cooking the hake steaks, scatter the stoned green olives over the fish and then cover the dish with aluminium foil.

4 Place the hake in a preheated oven at 160°C/325°F/Gas Mark 3. Cook for approximately 35–40 minutes until the fish is tender. Serve the steaks with a selection of freshly cooked vegetables.

VARIATION

Remove the fish from the marinade and dust with seasoned flour. Cook in oil or clarified butter until golden. Warm through the marinade, but do not boil, and serve as a sauce with lemon slices.

Dover Sole à la Meunière

Dover sole à la meunière, or 'in the style of a miller's wife', gets its name from the light dusting of flour that the fish is given before cooking.

NUTRITIONAL INFORMATION

Calories 584   Sugars 0g
Protein . . . . .74g   Fat 29g
Carbohydrate . . .10g   Saturates 14g

20 mins   15 mins

SERVES 4

I N G R E D I E N T S

4 tbsp plain flour

1 tsp salt

4 Dover soles, about 400 g/14 oz each,
  cleaned and skinned

150 g/5½ oz butter

3 tbsp lemon juice

1 tbsp chopped fresh parsley

¼ preserved lemon, finely chopped
  (optional)

salt and pepper

lemon wedges and parsley, to garnish

1 Mix the flour with the salt and place on a large plate or tray. Drop the soles into the flour, one at a time, and shake well to remove any excess. Melt 3 tablespoons of the butter in a small saucepan and use to brush the fish liberally all over.

2 Place under a preheated hot grill and cook for 5 minutes on each side.

3 Meanwhile, melt the remaining butter in a small pan. Pour cold water into a bowl, large enough to take the bottom of the pan. Keep nearby.

4 Heat the butter until it turns a golden brown and begins to smell nutty.

Remove immediately from the heat and immerse the base of the pan in the cold water to stop the cooking.

5 Put the fish onto individual serving plates, drizzle with the lemon juice and sprinkle over the parsley, and preserved lemon if using. Season with salt and pepper. Pour over the browned butter and serve immediately, garnished with lemon wedges and parsley sprigs.

COOK'S TIP

If you have a large enough pan (or two) you can cook the floured fish in butter, if you prefer.

Stuffed Monkfish Tail

A very impressive-looking dish, which is simple to prepare. The fish is stuffed with herbs and wrapped in slices of Parma ham.

NUTRITIONAL INFORMATION

Calories	154	Sugars	.........0g
Protein	........24g	Fat	...........6g
Carbohydrate	....0g	Saturates	.......1g

15 mins   40 mins

SERVES 6

I N G R E D I E N T S

750 g/1 lb 10 oz monkfish tail, skinned and trimmed

6 slices Parma ham

4 tbsp chopped fresh mixed herbs such as parsley, chives, basil and sage

1 tsp finely grated lemon zest

2 tbsp olive oil

salt and pepper

TO SERVE

shredded stir-fried vegetables

freshly cooked new potatoes

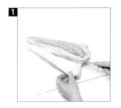

1 Using a sharp knife, carefully cut down each side of the central bone of the monkfish to leave 2 fillets. Wash and dry the fillets.

2 Lay the Parma ham slices widthways on a clean work surface so that they overlap slightly. Lay the fish fillets lengthways on top of the Parma ham so that the two cut sides face each other.

3 Mix together the chopped herbs and lemon zest. Season well. Pack this mixture onto the cut surface of one monkfish fillet. Press the 2 fillets together and wrap tightly with the Parma ham slices. Secure with string or cocktail sticks.

4 Heat the olive oil in a large, ovenproof frying pan and place the fish in the pan, seam-side down first, and brown the wrapped monkfish tail all over.

5 Transfer to a preheated oven and bake at 200°C/400°F/Gas Mark 6 for 25 minutes until the fish is golden and tender. Remove from the oven and leave to rest for 10 minutes before slicing thickly. Serve with shredded stir-fried vegetables and freshly cooked new potatoes.

COOK'S TIP

It is possible to remove the central bone from a monkfish tail without separating the two fillets completely. This makes it easier to stuff, but takes some practice.

Swordfish à la Maltaise

The firm texture of swordfish means it is often simply grilled, but it also lends itself to this delicate technique of cooking in a paper parcel.

NUTRITIONAL INFORMATION

Calories	303	Sugars	........10g
Protein	........34g	Fat	..........13g
Carbohydrate	...13g	Saturates	.......3g

35 mins   30 mins

SERVES 4

I N G R E D I E N T S

1 tbsp fennel seeds

2 tbsp fruity extra-virgin olive oil, plus extra for brushing and drizzling

2 large onions, thinly sliced

1 small garlic clove, crushed

4 swordfish steaks, about 175 g/6 oz each

1 large lemon, cut in half

2 large sun-ripened tomatoes, finely chopped

4 sprigs of fresh thyme

salt and pepper

1 Place the fennel seeds in a dry frying pan over a medium-high heat and toast, stirring, until they give off their aroma, watching carefully that they do not burn. Immediately tip them out of the frying pan onto a plate. Set aside.

2 Heat 2 tablespoons of olive oil in the frying pan. Add the onions and cook for 5 minutes, stirring occasionally. Add the garlic and continue cooking the onions until very soft and tender, but not brown. Remove the frying pan from the heat.

3 Cut out four 30-cm/12-inch circles of baking paper. Very lightly brush the centre of each paper circle with olive oil. Divide the onions and garlic between the circles, flattening them out to about the size of the fish steaks.

4 Top the onions in each parcel with a swordfish steak. Squeeze lemon juice over the fish steaks and drizzle with a little olive oil. Spoon the tomatoes over the top, add a sprig of thyme to each and season with salt and pepper to taste.

5 Fold the edges of the baking paper together, scrunching them tightly so that no cooking juices escape during cooking. Place the paper parcels on a baking tray and bake in a preheated oven at 200°C/400°F/Gas Mark 6 for 20 minutes.

6 To test if the fish is cooked, open one parcel and pierce the flesh with a knife – it should flake easily. Serve straight from the paper parcels.